THE WORKPLACE INVESTIGATION HANDBOOK

A Practitioner's Standard

Benjamin Davies

The Analytical Studio

First edition 2026

Published by The Analytical Studio

Victoria, Australia

theanalyticalstudio.com.au

ISBN: 978-1-7647169-0-1 (Paperback)

ISBN: 978-1-7647169-1-8 (eBook)

This methodology was built from a career of investigations that had real consequences for real people.

The standard it describes is the one that made findings defensible when challenged.

Contents

Author's Introduction

Why This Handbook Exists

Most workplace investigations are conducted by HR practitioners who have never been formally trained to conduct them.

This is not a criticism. The reality of HR practice in Australia is that the responsibility for investigating complaints falls to people whose training was in employee relations, organisational psychology, industrial law, or business management, and whose investigative methodology is what they have absorbed through experience, borrowed protocol, and the institutional memory of the organisations they have worked in. They are competent professionals applying their best judgment to a process that has not been taught to them in any formal sense, under time pressure, while managing the expectations and distress of multiple parties simultaneously.

The cost of this gap is recorded in the Fair Work Commission's decisions. Investigations that produced the wrong finding because the alternative explanation was not tested. Investigations that produced the right finding through a process that could not survive scrutiny when challenged. Investigations that complied with every procedural step on paper and failed every test of substance when the evidence was assessed at hearing. The methodology was missing, and the consequences fell on the parties whose working lives the investigations were supposed to address fairly.

This handbook exists to supply the missing standard. It is built from a career of investigative and prosecutorial practice, the research base in cognitive and health psychology that supports it, and the body of Fair

Work Commission decisions that has, over the past several years, become clearer and more consistent than at any prior point about what a defensible investigation requires.

The handbook's central claim is straightforward: there is a standard, it can be stated, it can be applied, and the gap between what an organisation knows it should be doing and what its investigations actually produce is almost always a methodology problem rather than a resource one. The chapters that follow describe the methodology. Each chapter establishes one stage of the investigation and the structural elements that make that stage work in practice rather than only in principle.

The handbook is written for a broad practitioner audience: HR professionals in private sector organisations, council HR teams, public sector investigators, small business owners who find themselves conducting investigations because no one else can, and the lawyers and consultants who advise them. The methodology is the same in every context. The proportionality of its application varies with the complexity of the matter and the resources available. The standard does not vary.

Three things this handbook is not. It is not a substitute for legal advice on specific matters; complex investigations should have appropriate legal support and the handbook does not replace it. It is not an exhaustive treatment of every possible workplace investigation scenario. And it is not a static document; the Fair Work Commission's decisions evolve, the Model Codes of Practice are revised, and the practitioner who relies on this handbook in five years should verify the currency of the specific authorities it cites while continuing to apply the methodology those authorities illustrate.

What follows is the standard a workplace investigation must meet, and the methodology that makes meeting it possible across the range of matters a practitioner will encounter.

A Note on Case Law

The Fair Work Commission decisions cited throughout this handbook were current at the time of writing. The methodology they illustrate, the investigative standard, the procedural fairness obligations, the evidentiary requirements, is derived from principles that have been consistently applied across Australian workplace law for decades and is unlikely to change materially. The specific cases may be superseded, distinguished, or supplemented by decisions handed down after this edition was prepared.

Practitioners are encouraged to verify the currency of any cited decision before relying on it in a specific matter, and to search the Fair Work Commission's decision database at fwc.gov.au for more recent authority on the specific question they are addressing. The methodology this handbook describes will remain sound regardless of what the Commission decides next. The cases are illustrations of the standard, not the standard itself.

A Note on Jurisdiction

The methodology described in this handbook is grounded in principles that apply to workplace investigations in any jurisdiction. The investigative standard, the alternative hypothesis test, the procedural fairness framework, the credibility assessment discipline, the structural separation between investigator and decision-maker, the management of evidence and its assessment, the construction of defensible findings and reports: these elements are not jurisdictionally bounded. They are the foundations of fair workplace investigation as a practice.

The legislative citations in this handbook are Australian. The Fair Work Act 2009 (Cth), the Work Health and Safety Act 2011 (Cth), the Occupational Health and Safety Act 2004 (Vic), the Privacy Act 1988 (Cth), the Charter of Human Rights and Responsibilities Act 2006 (Vic), and the Model Code of Practice on Managing Psychosocial Hazards are cited throughout because they form the regulatory framework within which the methodology operates in the jurisdiction the author practises in.

Practitioners working in other jurisdictions should substitute the equivalent statutory, regulatory, and adjudicative authorities for their own legal system: employment statutes, work health and safety legislation, privacy and human rights instruments, the relevant tribunal or court decisions, and the codes of practice or guidance issued by the relevant regulator. The methodology will apply. The specific authorities through which it is enforced will not be the same. Where this handbook describes obligations that arise under specific Australian instruments, practitioners outside Australia should read those passages as descriptions of obligations that almost certainly arise under equivalent instruments in their own jurisdiction, and verify the form those obligations take locally before applying them. The principle is universal. The expression is local.

Chapter One

The Investigative Standard

The complaint arrived on a Tuesday morning. Two sentences in an email, forwarded by a manager who added four words of her own: thought you should know. By the time the HR adviser opened it, the office already knew something was happening. Nobody had said anything officially. Nobody needed to.

This is where most workplace investigations begin. Not with a formal brief, a clear scope, or a defined methodology. With a forwarded email, an uncomfortable conversation, and the immediate pressure to do something. What happens in the next thirty minutes tends to shape everything that follows. The investigator who, in that thirty minutes, sends a holding message to the complainant, opens a file, and resists the pressure to ask the respondent for their side of the story before the scope of the matter is even understood is conducting an investigation. The investigator who returns the call, listens sympathetically, asks the respondent what happened, and forms an early view is producing the evidence on which a later complaint to the Fair Work Commission will be partly based.

The stated problem, in this scenario and in almost every workplace investigation that reaches a formal stage, is the complaint itself. Something happened. Someone was harmed. The organisation needs to find out what occurred and respond appropriately. That framing is not wrong. But it is incomplete, and the incompleteness is where investigations fail.

The real constraint is almost never a shortage of information. It is a shortage of method. Most HR practitioners who conduct workplace investigations have never been formally trained to do so. They proceed on instinct, on borrowed protocol, on a vague sense of what fairness requires, and on the assumption that if they listen carefully and document diligently, the truth will surface. Sometimes it does. More often, the investigation produces a finding that reflects what the investigator was inclined to believe before the first interview began, dressed in the language of process.

This handbook exists because that outcome is not inevitable. It is the product of a missing standard, and a missing standard can be supplied.

What a Standard Actually Means

In my career of investigative and prosecutorial practice, the most useful discipline I encountered was also the simplest to state and the hardest to apply consistently: a finding is not a finding until every alternative explanation has been considered and assessed against the evidence.

Not assumed away. Not left unexamined because the preferred explanation seems obvious. Considered, tested, and assessed.

The Davies Diagnostic, the foundational methodology of this series, applies this principle to organisational diagnosis: most organisations are working hard on the wrong problem because nobody told them to check the alternatives. In the workplace investigation context the principle operates as a specific and demanding test. Before an investigator concludes that conduct occurred, they must be able to articulate the strongest alternative explanation for the available evidence and demonstrate, with reference to that evidence, why that alternative is less supported than the finding they are reaching. Before they conclude that conduct did not occur, they must apply the same test in the other direction.

This is the investigative standard. It is not a criminal standard, and it is not a higher bar than the law requires. The civil standard of proof, the balance of probabilities, applies to workplace investigations in Australia. Section 387 of the Fair Work Act 2009 establishes the criteria against which the Fair Work Commission assesses whether a dismissal was harsh, unjust or unreasonable, and those criteria include whether there was a valid reason for the dismissal and whether the employee had a genuine opportunity to respond to it. The investigative standard concerns the quality of reasoning that produces a finding at the balance of probabilities threshold, not the threshold itself. A finding is defensible when the reasoning that produced it has tested the alternatives rather than preferred one account over another. Defensible means it holds up when challenged by the person with the strongest interest in disproving it.

One structural point before proceeding: the investigator is a fact-finder. Their role is to gather evidence, assess it against the investigative standard, and produce findings that a decision-maker can act upon. The investigator does not determine the outcome for the parties. That distinction matters because it defines what the investigation is for, and Chapters Eight and Nine of this handbook return to it in detail. For now, the point is this: a finding that is defensible protects the investigation, the decision-maker who relies on it, and the organisation that acts on it.

The Stated Problem and the Real Constraint

Consider what the forwarded email actually creates for the HR adviser who opens it. There is a complaint. There is a complainant. There is, by implication, a respondent. The organisation expects something to happen. The manager who forwarded the email expects to be updated. The complainant, who has taken a personal risk in making a formal report, expects to be heard. The respondent, who may not yet know a complaint exists, will shortly expect to be treated fairly.

None of these expectations are unreasonable. All of them create pressure, and pressure has a predictable effect on reasoning. It narrows it. The investigator managing the expectations of multiple stakeholders, conducting interviews, reviewing documents, and drafting findings under time pressure is not in the cognitive conditions that produce careful alternative-hypothesis testing. They are in the conditions that produce a conclusion formed early and confirmed by the evidence that supports it.

This is confirmation bias operating in a professional context. Pausing on what it actually feels like, before naming it, is more useful than the term itself. The investigator has received a complaint. One party's account is detailed, consistent, and distressing. The other party's account is defensive. The documents that have been provided support the complainant's timeline. The conclusion is forming before the first round of interviews is complete, and it feels like clarity. It feels like the evidence is doing its job. The problem is that this feeling of clarity is what confirmation bias produces. In Thinking, Fast and Slow, Kahneman identifies the specific mechanism: under pressure, the brain defaults to fast, pattern-matching cognition (System 1) rather than slow, deliberate analysis (System 2). It constructs a coherent narrative from the available information and stops looking for what is missing. The investigator who has not been given a structured methodology to apply does not avoid this default. They do not notice it happening.

The most common expression of this failure in workplace investigations is not the investigator who ignores evidence. It is the investigator who, faced with two conflicting accounts and no independent witness, treats the conflict itself as unresolvable. The accounts are characterised as misaligned. One person says it happened. The other says it did not. The finding is recorded as unable to be substantiated, not because the evidence has been assessed but because the assessment has been avoided. The Fair Work Commission identified this error directly.

In *Courtney Sewell v dnata Airport Services Pty Limited* [2025] FWC 2823, the Commission found that an allegation can be substantiated on the balance of probabilities even in the absence of a witness or recording, where the evidence as a whole, including the complainant's contemporaneous emotional state and immediate disclosure to colleagues, supports it. The absence of corroboration is evidence to be weighed. It is not a reason to stop weighing.

The investigative standard is the structural intervention that makes the default visible. It requires the investigator to pause at precisely the moments when the pressure to move quickly is highest: when the evidence seems to point clearly in one direction, when one party's account is vivid and compelling, when the conclusion feels obvious. Those are the moments when the alternative hypothesis matters most.

A reasonable objection at this point is that this standard sounds more demanding than most practitioners can realistically apply. The objection deserves a direct answer. The standard is demanding. It does not, however, require more information or more time. It requires a specific question asked at a specific point in the reasoning process: what is the strongest explanation for this evidence other than the one I am reaching, and what would the evidence look like if that alternative were true? Asking that question before writing a finding takes minutes. Defending a finding that did not ask it can take considerably longer.

The handbook is designed around this asymmetry. Every structured element it introduces, the evidence matrix in Chapter Four, the cognitive interview framework in Chapter Six, the six-component finding architecture in Chapter Eight, exists to make the alternative hypothesis test routinely possible rather than heroically demanding. The standard is high. The scaffolding the handbook provides is what makes the height sustainable across an investigation programme rather than achievable only on the matters that already have the right outcome built into them.

The Legal and Safety Framework

The investigative standard does not exist in isolation. It operates within a legal and regulatory framework that practitioners need to understand before the first interview begins.

The Fair Work Act 2009 (Cth) is the primary legislative instrument governing workplace investigations that may result in disciplinary action or dismissal. Section 387 establishes the criteria the Commission applies when assessing whether a dismissal was harsh, unjust or unreasonable. These criteria include whether there was a valid reason for the dismissal related to the person's conduct, whether the person was notified of that reason, whether they were given a genuine opportunity to respond, and whether any other relevant matters bear on the fairness of the process. An investigation that does not meet the standard establishes the conditions for a finding that fails every one of these criteria at once.

The Work Health and Safety Act 2011 (Cth) and the Occupational Health and Safety Act 2004 (Vic) impose a positive duty on organisations to ensure, so far as is reasonably practicable, the psychological health and safety of workers. This duty does not pause during a workplace investigation. It intensifies. The people inside an investigation, as complainants, respondents, and witnesses, are workers whose health and safety the organisation has a legal obligation to protect. An investigation that causes psychological harm through procedural injustice, unnecessary delay, breach of confidentiality, or contempt for the dignity of the parties is not just a poorly conducted investigation. For practitioners in the public sector in particular, it may constitute a breach of a statutory duty.

The Charter of Human Rights and Responsibilities Act 2006 (Vic) applies to public authorities in Victoria. It protects the right to privacy and reputation, the right to a fair hearing before an independent and impartial decision-maker, and the right to be treated with dignity and humanity. Section 38 makes it unlawful for a public authority to act incompatibly with these rights. Council HR teams and public sector practitioners conducting investigations are not exercising a discretion when they apply these standards. They are fulfilling a legal obligation, and their process must be demonstrably compatible with these rights if it is ever examined.

Together these frameworks establish that a workplace investigation is not a purely internal administrative process. It is a formal exercise of institutional power over people's working lives, reputations, and psychological health. The investigative standard is the practitioner's method for exercising that power responsibly.

Why Psychological Safety is an Evidentiary Requirement

An investigation conducted in an environment of psychological threat does not produce better evidence under pressure. It produces worse evidence, and the practitioner cannot know which parts of an account are accurate and which are the product of a witness managing their own anxiety rather than retrieving their memory.

This is not a pastoral observation. It is a finding from cognitive psychology with direct implications for investigative method.

When a witness is anxious or fearful, their working memory capacity is reduced. Working memory is the cognitive system that supports active recall: the ability to hold a partial account in mind, search for additional detail, and construct a coherent narrative from fragmentary memory. Under conditions of high arousal, the brain prioritises immediate threat-relevant processing over this slower, more effortful retrieval. The witness becomes less able to do the thing the investigator needs them to do. The Yerkes-Dodson principle (Yerkes and Dodson, 1908), established and replicated across more than a century of cognitive psychology research, shows that performance on complex cognitive tasks degrades when arousal is too high. That is the normal condition of a witness in a formal workplace investigation who has not been put at ease.

The specific behaviours this produces are well-documented. Witnesses who feel psychologically unsafe during an interview are more likely to withhold information, to provide abbreviated answers rather than full accounts, to stop volunteering unsolicited but relevant detail, and in some cases to guess at answers in order to terminate an interaction that has become distressing. None of these behaviours are immediately visible to the investigator as responses to psychological threat. They present as incomplete accounts, as evasiveness, or as apparent lack of credibility. The investigator who does not understand the mechanism draws the wrong conclusions from the evidence, because they are reading the product of the interview environment rather than the product of the witness's actual memory.

The cognitive interview methodology developed by Fisher and Geiselman (1992), which underpins Chapter Six of this handbook, is built on the inverse of this problem. Psychological safety is not a precondition that must be achieved before the real work of interviewing begins. It is the mechanism through which reliable testimony is produced. An interview conducted with genuine rapport, with control transferred to the witness, with open-ended questions that allow uninterrupted narrative, produces a qualitatively different account from the same person in the same room. Not because the witness has become more honest. Because they have become more able to retrieve accurately.

The Fair Work Commission reached the same conclusion from a different direction. In *Roy Smout v BHP Coal Pty Ltd* [2024] FWC 2062, Commissioner Riordan found that the investigation's use of telephone interviews for complainants was totally inappropriate because body language is an essential component of every interview. The Commission found the investigator's use of leading questions to be evidence of a lack of investigative rigour that undermined the reliability of the findings. The Commission was not making a welfare argument. It was making an evidentiary one: the method produced unreliable results, and the employer had acted on them.

The people inside a workplace investigation are not evidence sources. They are people whose working lives, reputations, and psychological health may be permanently altered by what this process produces. The investigator who treats them as such obtains better evidence as a direct consequence, not as a reward for good intentions.

The Operating Question

Most workplace investigations begin with a question that sounds right but is not precise enough to do the work required of it: what happened?

What happened is the right destination. It is not the right question to navigate by.

Every chapter of this handbook is oriented around a different question: what is the most reliable explanation for what the evidence shows?

The difference is not semantic. What happened invites narrative. It positions the investigator as the recipient of accounts, weighing one story against another and deciding which is more credible. What is the most reliable explanation for what the evidence shows positions the investigator as an analyst. The accounts are evidence. The documents are evidence. The absence of expected evidence is evidence. The investigator's task is not to decide who to believe. It is to assess what the available evidence, taken as a whole, most reliably supports, and whether any alternative explanation is more consistent with that evidence than the finding being reached.

This reframing has a practical consequence that runs through every stage of the investigation: it changes what the practitioner is looking for. An investigator asking what happened gathers accounts. An investigator asking what is the most reliable explanation for what the evidence shows gathers accounts, tests them against documentary evidence, identifies corroboration and inconsistency, considers alternative explanations, and produces a finding that can be stated in terms of what it is based on and why the alternatives were less supported.

The two questions also produce different relationships with the parties. The investigator who is deciding who to believe is in an evaluative posture toward people who can feel they are being evaluated, and who respond accordingly. The investigator who is assessing what the evidence most reliably supports is in an analytical posture toward a body of material, of which the parties' accounts are an important part but not the totality. The first posture invites the parties to perform credibility. The second invites them to provide information. The quality of what is obtained differs accordingly.

The second type of investigation is harder to conduct. It is also the only type that produces findings worth relying on.

PRACTITIONER NOTE

The most common failure this chapter is designed to address is not the investigation that goes badly wrong. It is the investigation that appears to go well, produces a finding, and then does not survive the scrutiny of a Fair Work Commission application, an internal appeal, or a conversation with a lawyer representing one of the parties.

These investigations fail not because the investigator was careless but because they were applying the wrong standard without knowing it. They were asking what happened and gathering enough evidence to answer that question to their own satisfaction. They were not asking what is the most reliable explanation for what the evidence shows, and testing the alternatives before finalising any finding.

The specific experience from an investigative and prosecutorial background is that this failure is almost invisible until it is too late. The investigation feels thorough because substantial work has been done. The finding feels justified because the evidence that supports it is real. The problem is the evidence that was not tested, the alternative explanation that was not articulated, and the finding that went further than what the evidence actually supported.

There is a second failure this chapter is designed to prevent, and it is the one that arrives quietly rather than dramatically. The investigation that treats conflicting accounts as automatically unresolvable. The finding recorded as unsubstantiated not because the evidence has been assessed but because the assessment felt impossible when two people said different things and there was nobody else in the room. That is not a finding. That is an abdication dressed as one. The evidence still has to be assessed. The alternative hypothesis still has to be tested. The balance of probabilities still has to be applied, even in the absence of a witness, even in the absence of documents, even when the only available evidence is two conflicting accounts and the pattern of behaviour surrounding them.

The alternative hypothesis question, asked before writing any conclusion, is the practical discipline this handbook installs. It does not guarantee the right finding. Nothing does. It does guarantee that the finding was reached rather than defaulted to, and that is the difference between a defensible investigation and an expensive one.

A NOTE ON COGNITIVE STYLE

The structured approach in this handbook, the evidence matrix, the investigation plan, the section-by-section report template, the credibility framework, was not designed primarily for practitioners who find structure easy. It was designed for the reality of how investigations are actually conducted: under time pressure, with incomplete information, while managing the competing needs of multiple parties, and often without formal training in investigative methodology.

For practitioners who think in non-linear patterns, who generate connections quickly and reconstruct sequences with effort, the explicit structure here serves a specific function. It holds the state of the investigation in a visible, navigable form so that the investigator does not have to. The evidence matrix does not replace analytical capacity. It externalises the evidential map so that capacity can be directed at assessment rather than at remembering what has already been gathered.

Investigative interviewing draws on two distinct types of cognitive labour. The components requiring heavy, sequential working memory often demand targeted structural support for minds that don't naturally think in a straight line. However, the open-ended, relational aspects of interviewing are where a non-linear cognitive style excels. This processing depth is a major asset for complex investigations: it thrives on advanced pattern recognition, catches the inconsistencies that linear frameworks filter out, reads the 'blank spaces' or omissions in a narrative, and comfortably holds multiple conflicting theories at once without collapsing them too early. There are all kinds of cognitive experience that present differently in different people and at different times. This handbook is not designed for a particular cognitive profile. It is designed to work well regardless of the one you have, because the structure is the scaffold, not the ceiling.

What Comes Next

The investigative standard is established in this chapter because every procedural step that follows only makes sense in relation to it. Receiving and scoping a complaint is the process of defining what question the investigation will answer. Planning the investigation is the process of determining how the evidence needed to answer it will be gathered. Conducting interviews, assessing evidence, and making findings are the process of applying the standard to what the investigation has produced.

The standard is demanding. The work the standard describes is cognitively heavy, conducted under institutional pressure, and carried by practitioners who are usually managing more than one matter at a time. The handbook is constructed on the premise that the standard is sustainable when the method is explicit and the scaffolding is in place. Where the standard appears to require more than is realistic, that is almost always a signal that the structural support has not yet been built, not that the standard should be lowered. The chapters that follow build the scaffolding.

The standard does not change across these stages. What is the most reliable explanation for what the evidence shows, and has every significant alternative been considered and assessed? Those two questions, asked consistently and answered honestly, are what the rest of this handbook is built to support.

Chapter Two

Receiving a Complaint

The manager appeared in the doorway at 4:47 on a Friday afternoon.

She did not sit down. She said she needed to tell the HR adviser something before the weekend, something that had been building for a while, something she thought HR should probably know about. The account that followed was detailed in some places and vague in others, circled back on itself twice, and arrived at a conclusion that had been formed before she walked through the door: the respondent needed to go.

By 5:15 the HR adviser had received what felt like a complete picture. A named complainant, a named respondent, a series of incidents spanning several months, and an implicit instruction about the outcome. What the HR adviser had not received, and would not recognise the absence of until much later, was a complaint. What had been received was a manager's interpretation of a situation, filtered through her own interests and her own conclusions, delivered at the moment of maximum time pressure, in the format least conducive to careful thought.

The HR practitioner who accepts the manager's conclusion at the door is not saving time. They are outsourcing their judgment to the person most likely to be wrong.

This is how most workplace investigations actually begin. Not with a formal written complaint, a clearly defined allegation, or a considered request for investigation. With a conversation that creates momentum before a scope has been defined, a timeline has been established, or a single question has been asked about whether a formal investigation is the right response at all.

What happens in that first conversation determines more about the investigation's outcome than any subsequent step. Not because the first conversation produces evidence, but because it produces a frame. The frame shapes every interview, every document request, and every credibility assessment that follows. An investigation that begins with the wrong frame produces findings that answer the wrong question, and findings that answer the wrong question do not survive scrutiny regardless of how carefully the process was followed.

The First Decision: Receive, Not Begin

The most important discipline in receiving a complaint is understanding what receiving it does not authorise.

Receiving a complaint authorises the organisation to take the complaint seriously. It authorises the HR practitioner to ask enough questions to understand what is being alleged and who is involved. It authorises a preliminary assessment of whether the matter requires formal investigation, informal resolution, referral to another body, or some other response entirely. It does not authorise the investigation to begin.

This distinction matters because the investigation begins the moment the practitioner starts forming a view about what happened. The moment the practitioner silently assesses the complainant's credibility. The moment they consider whether the alleged conduct sounds like something the named respondent would do. The moment the frame is set. An investigator who has formed a view before the first formal interview has already compromised the most important output the investigation is designed to produce: a finding reached by a defined process rather than confirmed by one.

The natural counterargument here is that a pause feels like delay when a manager is standing in the doorway expecting action. The counterargument is understandable and wrong. The pause is not delay. It is the work. An investigation that begins without a defined scope, a proportionality assessment, and a conflict of interest check has not started faster. It has accumulated a debt that compounds at every stage, and the compounding accelerates when the finding is challenged.

Receiving a complaint therefore requires a specific discipline that runs against the natural grain of professional competence. The impulse of a skilled HR practitioner is to problem-solve: to assess, to categorise, to begin forming a response. That impulse needs to be suspended at the intake stage and replaced with a more limited set of questions. What is being alleged? When and where did it occur? Who are the parties? Is there any safety risk that requires action before a formal process begins? Everything else waits until the Terms of Reference have been defined.

The practical expression of this discipline is the intake record: a written note of the complaint as received, before any assessment has been applied to it. Not a summary of what the practitioner thought was significant. Not a record of the practitioner's initial impressions. The account as given, in the terms in which it was given, with the date, time, and circumstances of the conversation noted. This document serves two functions. It preserves the complaint in its original form so that scope creep can be identified later. And it creates a moment of deliberate pause between receiving and assessing, which is the moment the investigation's integrity is either established or compromised.

The Preliminary Assessment: Four Questions Before Terms of Reference Are Set

Before an investigation is scoped, four questions must be answered. The answers determine not just what the investigation covers but whether a formal investigation is the appropriate response at all.

Is this matter within the organisation's jurisdiction to investigate?

Not every complaint that arrives on an HR practitioner's desk is a matter the organisation is obliged or entitled to investigate. The Fair Work Act 2009 creates specific jurisdictions, and conduct that falls outside the employment relationship, that occurred before the relevant employment period, or that is already the subject of proceedings in another forum may not be appropriate for internal investigation. The Work Health and Safety Act 2011 creates obligations around psychosocial hazards that may require a WHS response running parallel to or instead of a disciplinary investigation. The preliminary assessment must include a considered judgment about what the organisation is legally empowered to investigate and what it is legally required to investigate, because these are not always the same thing.

Before proceeding, the practitioner should also map the external bodies that may have a concurrent or overlapping jurisdiction in the matter. A bullying complaint may engage WorkSafe's WHS jurisdiction. A sexual harassment complaint may give rise to a complaint to the Australian Human Rights Commission or its state equivalent. Conduct that may constitute a criminal offence engages the obligation to refer to police, which is independent of whether the complainant has done so. For public sector practitioners, the integrity commission's jurisdiction, the relevant ombudsman, the public interest disclosure framework, and sector-specific regulators may also apply. The mapping exercise is not legal advice. It is a structural awareness step that determines what questions need to be answered before the internal investigation can proceed without compromising or being compromised by an external process. Where an external process is already underway or appears likely to commence, the practitioner should seek specific advice before proceeding beyond preliminary steps, because findings produced through an internal investigation may not survive scrutiny in an external forum that applies different evidentiary standards.

What type of conduct is alleged, and what is the appropriate process?

Workplace complaints are not uniform, and the same process does not serve all of them equally. The first assessment of conduct type must apply an objective test: would a reasonable person, knowing what is known at the intake stage, consider the alleged behaviour unreasonable? This is the threshold the Stop Bullying Benchbook applies, and it is the correct starting point because it prevents the assessment from being driven by the complainant's subjective experience of distress alone. Distress is not the standard. The conduct is the standard.

Having applied the objective test, the proportionality assessment follows. A complaint about a single incident between two colleagues with no prior history may be better resolved through a facilitated conversation than a formal investigation. A complaint about a pattern of conduct that has continued over months, involves a power imbalance, or has created a health and safety risk requires a formal process. A complaint that describes conduct potentially constituting a criminal offence requires an immediate assessment of whether the matter should be referred to police before or instead of an internal investigation proceeding. The Model Code of Practice on Managing Psychosocial Hazards is explicit: the investigation must be proportionate to the level of risk and complexity. A formal investigation applied to a matter that does not warrant it causes harm to all parties without producing better findings.

The political and symbolic dimensions of the complaint also require assessment at this stage, even if they cannot be fully resolved. Who has an interest in a particular outcome? What story is the organisation already telling itself about this conduct or these parties? These questions do not determine the investigation's direction. Ignoring them leaves the practitioner unprepared for the pressures that will arrive later.

Is there an immediate safety risk requiring action before the investigation begins?

Some complaints describe conduct creating an ongoing risk to the health and safety of the complainant, the respondent, or other workers. That risk does not wait for the investigation to conclude. An organisation that receives a complaint describing serious harassment and takes no interim protective measures while the investigation proceeds has failed its positive duty to prevent psychological harm regardless of what the investigation eventually finds. The positive duty, established under both the WHS Act and the Sex Discrimination Act, requires organisations to take reasonable and proportionate measures to eliminate, as far as possible, the risk of harm, not merely to respond to harm after it has occurred.

Interim measures might include temporary changes to reporting lines, work locations, or rosters. They might include a stand-down of the respondent, handled with the sensitivity the psychosocial hazard code requires: privately, with care for the working relationship, and without implying a predetermined outcome. The stand-down is communicated to the respondent as a risk control measure, not a finding. That distinction must be stated explicitly, because a respondent who understands the stand-down as an implied finding of guilt has grounds for a procedural fairness complaint before the investigation has conducted a single interview.

How the stand-down is communicated internally is as consequential as how it is communicated to the respondent. A stand-down explained to the team as a routine matter pending an investigation is a procedural step. A stand-down accompanied by visible reassignment of the respondent's work, exclusion from team communications, or commentary from the manager about what the organisation will not tolerate is a finding announced before the investigation has begun. The respondent who returns after the investigation has not substantiated the allegations faces a workplace that has already drawn its conclusion, and the organisation faces a risk that was avoidable.

Who should conduct this investigation?

The investigator must have the confidence of all parties, sufficient seniority and independence to withstand pressure from within the organisation, and the skills to conduct a procedurally fair process. Critically, the investigator must be distinct from the person who will make the disciplinary decision. The investigator's role is to find facts and produce a report. The decision-maker's role is to determine what action, if any, those findings warrant. Conflating these roles compromises the integrity of both.

Conflict of interest in investigator selection is frequently a matter of optics as much as substance. A practitioner who has a personal relationship with either party, who reports to a manager implicated in the complaint, or who has already expressed a view about the matter must recuse themselves, because the appearance of bias is sufficient to undermine the investigation even if the bias does not affect the outcome. When an impartial internal investigator cannot be identified, an external investigator should be engaged. This is not an admission of incapacity. It is the appropriate response to a structural conflict, and the failure to recognise and act on that conflict is one of the most consistently identified sources of procedurally vulnerable investigations in Fair Work Commission proceedings.

The conflict of interest threshold operates with particular force in small organisations and resource-constrained environments. In a small business where the HR practitioner knows both parties personally, in a council where the investigator, the relevant manager, and the decision-maker are all known to each other and all subject to the political dynamics of an elected institution, or in a small public sector agency where the reporting structure makes apparent independence difficult to establish, the test is not whether internal investigation is operationally convenient. It is whether a fair-minded observer would reasonably apprehend that the available internal investigator might not bring an impartial mind to the matter. Where the available investigator cannot satisfy that external standard, external investigation should be considered mandatory regardless of cost. The cost of an internal investigation that produces a finding the Commission sets aside on grounds of apprehended bias is greater, and it falls on the same organisation.

The Terms of Reference

The Terms of Reference is the document that defines what the investigation will examine, who holds the authority to conduct it, and what the investigator is being asked to produce. It is the most consequential document produced before any interview takes place, and in most investigations it receives less attention than any subsequent step.

The Terms of Reference must address several elements. The allegations being investigated, stated as specifically as the available information allows. The parties to the investigation. The relevant time period. Whether the investigator is being asked to make findings of fact only, or findings of fact and determinations about whether those facts constitute a breach of the relevant policy or code of conduct. The types of evidence that will be sought. And, explicitly, what is outside the scope of the investigation.

That last element is not a limitation. It is a protection. The practitioner who receives a complaint about three specific incidents and discovers in the course of interviewing that there are additional matters faces a specific decision about whether to expand the scope. Without defined Terms of Reference, that decision is made informally, inconsistently, and often under pressure from one or both parties. With defined Terms of Reference, the decision is made deliberately, documented, and communicated to all parties before the investigation proceeds further.

The Terms of Reference should be completed before the first formal interview is conducted and agreed with the person or body that commissioned the investigation. It does not need to be shared with the parties at the outset, but it needs to exist in writing so that the investigation has a defined question to answer and a defined authority to answer it. Chapter Four develops the investigation plan that operationalises this document. The Terms of Reference are the brief. The plan is the work.

The Complaint That Arrives Pre-Packaged

There is a specific internal experience that accompanies the well-organised complaint. The account is detailed and consistent. It is supported by documents the complainant has already gathered. A senior person in the organisation has signalled, before the formal process has begun, that they share the complainant's view. The conclusion is forming before the investigator has reviewed the first piece of independent evidence, and it feels like clarity rather than premature judgment. That feeling is the problem. The coherence of the account is doing the work that the evidence is supposed to do.

The complaint that arrives with its conclusion already attached takes several forms. The manager who delivers a complaint and an expected outcome simultaneously. The complainant who has documented their allegations in exhaustive detail with a suggested finding appended. The senior leader who contacts the HR adviser before the complaint has been formally received to explain why the respondent needs to go. The complaint that has been discussed with colleagues, refined across multiple conversations, and arrived at the practitioner's desk reflecting as much advocacy as recollection.

None of these situations mean the complaint is false. They mean the complaint has been through a process before it reached the investigation, and that process has shaped it. The political dimensions noted earlier are particularly relevant here: a complaint that has gathered institutional momentum has gathered institutional interests as well, and those interests will exert pressure on the investigation whether or not they are named. The practitioner's task is to receive what has been delivered, note the form in which it was delivered, and assess the allegation on the evidence rather than on the shape in which it arrived.

The discipline is uncomfortable because it requires the practitioner to actively hold open a question that already feels answered. Not to dismiss the complainant's account. Not to treat a well-organised complaint as suspect. To treat the account as the starting point for an evidence-based assessment rather than the conclusion that the evidence will confirm. The investigative standard, applied at its earliest and most demanding point, is the same question asked in every subsequent chapter: what is the most reliable explanation for what the evidence shows, and what would the evidence look like if the alternative were true?

Notifying the Parties

Once the preliminary assessment is complete, the Terms of Reference are defined, and the decision to proceed with a formal investigation has been made, both parties must be notified. The manner of that notification is the first concrete signal the investigation sends about whether the process can be trusted.

The complainant needs to know that their complaint has been received, that a formal investigation will proceed, what the scope covers, what the process will involve, and what support is available to them. They are entitled to this information as a matter of procedural fairness, not courtesy. A complainant who does not know what the investigation covers cannot assess whether their complaint has been taken seriously. A complainant who is not told what support is available may not seek it, and the organisation has a positive duty of care to their psychological health during the process.

The respondent needs to know that a complaint has been received and that an investigation will proceed. They are not, at this stage, entitled to the full detail of the allegations: that disclosure comes when they are formally interviewed and given a genuine opportunity to respond. What they are entitled to know is that a process is underway, what it involves, that they are presumed not to have engaged in the alleged conduct until the investigation finds otherwise, and what support is available to them. This includes the right to have a support person present at any discussions relating to potential disciplinary action. That right is established by s.387(d) of the Fair Work Act 2009, and it is a statutory requirement, not an optional offering. The notification must name it.

Both notifications should be made in writing, following the verbal notification, with a clear record of what was communicated and when. The written record protects the organisation and the parties. It also establishes the informational fairness baseline that the psychosocial hazard code's three pillars of organisational justice require: procedural justice through a fair process, informational fairness through keeping people appropriately informed, and interpersonal fairness through treating people with dignity and respect.

The *Courtney Sewell v dnata Airport Services Pty Limited* [2025] FWC 2823 decision demonstrates what happens when outcome communication at the end of an investigation fails in the same way intake communication can fail at the beginning. The outcome was communicated verbally before a written letter followed weeks later. The letter used language so ambiguous the complainant could not determine what had been found. The employer's subsequent handling of the complainant's return to work created conditions that the Commission found forced her resignation. The finding of constructive dismissal, and the $36,468.39 compensation that followed, traced directly to failures of communication and follow-through that the notification discipline established at the outset is designed to prevent.

When the Investigation Should Not Proceed

The preliminary assessment will sometimes produce a finding that a formal internal investigation is not the appropriate response. That outcome is not a failure of process. It is the process working correctly.

A complaint describing conduct that may constitute a criminal offence should be assessed against the question of police referral before internal investigation proceeds. Internal investigations do not have the coercive powers of a criminal inquiry, cannot compel production of evidence, and produce findings at the civil standard that may complicate a subsequent criminal process if conducted first.

A complaint about conduct falling within the organisation's WHS obligations may require a WHS investigation rather than a disciplinary one, or both running concurrently. The psychosocial hazard code of practice is explicit that organisations may need to conduct two concurrent processes: a disciplinary investigation into breaches of conduct standards, and a systematic WHS investigation to identify and control the hazards that created the conditions for the conduct. The concurrent WHS inquiry carries a duty to consult: under the Occupational Health and Safety Act 2004 (Vic), workers must have a reasonable opportunity to express their views on the hazard and its controls. That obligation runs alongside the investigation, not after it.

A practitioner who conducts only the disciplinary investigation and closes the file on a finding of unsubstantiated has not discharged the organisation's obligations. The underlying hazard may exist regardless of the finding about individual conduct.

A complaint describing a workplace conflict rather than a conduct breach may be better served by mediation or a facilitated conversation. Applying a formal investigation to a situation that does not require one causes disproportionate harm to all parties and produces a finding that addresses the stated problem rather than the real one. The preliminary assessment is the investigation's first diagnostic moment. Its output is not always proceed with formal investigation. Sometimes its output is this requires a different response, and reaching that conclusion through a structured assessment is exactly what the investigative standard requires.

PRACTITIONER NOTE

The specific failure pattern this chapter is designed to prevent is the investigation that begins before it has been defined.

The practitioner who moves from receiving a complaint to interviewing witnesses without Terms of Reference, a proportionality assessment, a conflict of interest check, and a notification protocol has not skipped administrative steps. They have skipped the steps that determine what the investigation is for and whether the findings it produces will be defensible.

The Friday afternoon conversation in this chapter's opening is not an unusual circumstance. It is the normal mode of complaint receipt in most organisations. The manager at the door, the account that arrives with its conclusion attached, the time pressure that makes careful thought feel like a luxury, these are the conditions under which most investigations begin, and the conditions under which most investigation failures are established.

The intake record, the preliminary assessment, the Terms of Reference, and the notification protocol are not bureaucratic requirements. They are the structure that makes it possible to conduct a fair investigation in unfair conditions. A practitioner who has defined Terms of Reference knows what evidence to gather. A practitioner who has completed a conflict of interest check knows who should not be the investigator. A practitioner who has made a proportionality judgment knows whether formal investigation is the right tool. A practitioner who has completed the notification protocol has given both parties the procedural foundation they are owed before the first interview begins.

The investigation that skips these steps does not save time. It borrows it, at a rate that compounds whenever the finding is challenged.

A NOTE ON COGNITIVE STYLE

The intake stage is cognitively demanding. It requires the practitioner to receive a detailed, emotionally weighted account and hold it without processing it to conclusion. For practitioners who generate connections and pattern-matches quickly, this is not intuitive. The account arrives and the picture starts forming before the first clarifying question has been asked. The alternative hypothesis is not a frame the mind naturally holds open when the primary narrative is coherent and compelling.

The intake record is the cognitive intervention for this stage. Writing the account down as received, before assessing it, creates a separation between reception and analysis. The record is not the analysis. It is the raw material the analysis will work from. Keeping those two things in separate documents, and in separate cognitive moments, is the practical discipline that prevents the intake conversation from becoming the finding.

The Terms of Reference serve the same function at a higher level. They externalise the question the investigation is designed to answer so that the investigation does not drift toward the question the intake conversation suggested. For practitioners who think non-linearly, a written Terms of Reference is not a constraint on the inquiry. It is the anchor that makes non-linear thinking productive rather than dispersive.

Two further points for practitioners working with parties who may be neurodivergent. First, the intake process for a neurodivergent complainant or witness may require adaptation: more time, written rather than verbal communication, or a different format for recording the account. The standard intake process was not designed with neurodivergent communication styles in mind, and applying it without adaptation risks producing an incomplete or inaccurate record before the investigation has begun. Second, if a respondent's neurodivergence is known or becomes apparent during the intake stage, the investigator should note it and consider how it may affect the respondent's capacity to engage with the process, both in terms of the support they may need and the adaptations the investigation should make when they are formally interviewed.

What Comes Next

The complaint has been received. The preliminary assessment is complete. The Terms of Reference are defined. The parties have been notified.

Chapter Three addresses the legal and procedural framework governing how the investigation proceeds from this point: natural justice, procedural fairness, and the specific obligations that the Fair Work Act and common law place on the investigation before the first formal interview begins. These obligations are not separate from the investigative standard. They are its legal expression, and understanding them before the investigation proceeds is not optional.

Chapter Three

Procedural Fairness

A show cause meeting scheduled for a Friday afternoon is not an invitation to respond. It is a request for the respondent to participate in their own dismissal.

The practitioner who scheduled that meeting knew, before it began, what the outcome would be. The letter was already drafted. The HR team was not available over the long weekend. The mine was transferring ownership in four days. The respondent was given a 5 to 10 minute notification meeting, a 30-minute break, and then a termination letter. A union delegate was present. A support person was named. Every procedural fairness box, on paper, was ticked.

The Fair Work Commission found the dismissal unfair.

Natural justice is not satisfied by the appearance of a fair process. It is satisfied by a fair process. The distinction sounds obvious until the pressure arrives, and the pressure always arrives. The organisation that needs a disciplinary process finalised before a long weekend. The manager who commissioned the investigation and needs an outcome before the matter becomes a performance management issue. The investigator who has already formed a view and needs to provide the respondent with an opportunity to confirm it. Each of these produces an investigation that looks procedurally compliant and is not.

The reasonable counterargument is that strict procedural standards create bureaucratic delay in situations requiring urgent action. The counterargument is understandable. The answer is that the urgency is almost always manufactured, and the organisations that manufacture it most consistently are the ones that accumulate Fair Work Commission applications most reliably. A process conducted properly takes longer. A finding that does not survive challenge costs more.

What Natural Justice Actually Requires

Natural justice is a common law principle with a long history and a simple core: people are entitled to know the case against them and to have a genuine opportunity to respond to it before a decision affecting their interests is made.

In the workplace investigation context it operates through two rules that are distinct in their application but connected in their purpose. The hearing rule requires that the respondent be informed of the allegations against them with enough detail to allow a meaningful response, that they be given a genuine opportunity to respond before any finding is made, and that the response be considered by the decision-maker before any action is taken. The bias rule requires that the person making the finding, and the person making the decision based on it, must not have a pre-existing interest in the outcome.

The legal test that gives both rules their practical consequence is the Burchell Test, drawn from established Fair Work Commission authority and applied consistently in Australian unfair dismissal proceedings. To demonstrate that a disciplinary process was fair, the employer must show three things. First, a genuine belief that the conduct occurred. Second, reasonable grounds for that belief. Third, a reasonable investigation conducted before the decision was made. All three elements are necessary, and they are not interchangeable. A genuine belief based on inadequate grounds is not sufficient. Reasonable grounds established without a reasonable investigation are not sufficient. The Burchell Test is the framework within which the investigative standard operates, and it is the framework the Commission will apply when assessing whether the process produced a defensible outcome.

Section 387 of the Fair Work Act 2009 gives the Commission its statutory authority to assess these questions. The criteria include whether there was a valid reason for the dismissal related to the person's conduct, whether the person was notified of that reason under s.387(b), whether they were given an opportunity to respond to that reason under s.387(c), and whether any other relevant matters bear on the fairness of the process. A failure on any criterion can render a technically correct finding legally indefensible.

The Charter of Human Rights and Responsibilities Act 2006 adds a further dimension for public sector practitioners in Victoria. Section 24 protects the right to a fair hearing before a competent, independent and impartial decision-maker. Section 13 protects the right to privacy and reputation from unlawful or arbitrary interference. Section 38 makes it unlawful for a public authority to act in a way incompatible with these rights. Council HR teams and other public sector practitioners are fulfilling a legal obligation when they apply natural justice standards, and their process must be demonstrably compatible with these rights if it is examined.

The procedural and distributive dimensions of justice are related but distinct. Natural justice governs the process: the fairness of the procedure through which the finding is reached. Distributive justice governs the outcome: the fairness of the consequence that follows a finding of misconduct. Both are relevant to the Commission's assessment of whether a dismissal was harsh, unjust or unreasonable. A fair process that produces a disproportionate consequence is still vulnerable to a finding of harshness. Both dimensions require the investigator's attention.

The Particularisation Requirement

The allegation that does not say enough is the most common procedural fairness failure in workplace investigations, and it almost always arrives as an attempt to avoid prejudging the outcome rather than an attempt to deny it.

The form the failure takes is specific. The respondent receives a letter notifying them that they are the subject of an investigation into alleged conduct that was inappropriate, offensive, or contrary to the organisation's values. Sometimes the letter names a policy that may have been breached. Occasionally it specifies a date. What it does not do is tell the respondent what they actually did, in enough detail that they can assess the allegation against their own recollection, identify witnesses who may be relevant, and prepare a response addressing the substance of the case against them.

The Commission's reasoning in cases following *Barclay v Nylex Corporation* establishes the standard precisely: a respondent who was not notified of the particulars of why they had been dismissed was denied the opportunity to respond that procedural fairness requires. The termination letter in *Roy Smout v BHP Coal Pty Ltd* [2024] FWC 2062 illustrates what adequate particularisation looks like: three allegations, each naming the date, location, and nature of the alleged conduct, and the specific policy said to have been breached. That level of detail allows the respondent to engage with the allegation rather than guess at it.

Put concretely, the difference between adequate and inadequate particularisation is the difference between two sentences. Inadequate: that on or around March, the respondent engaged in conduct toward Worker A that was contrary to the Code of Conduct. Adequate: that on 14 March 2024, in the Bay 3 maintenance bay between 0830 and 0900, the respondent made the comments to Worker A set out at paragraphs 6 to 8 of the allegation letter, in breach of clauses 4.2 and 4.3 of the Code of Conduct. The first version invites a defensive response with no traction on the actual conduct. The second invites a substantive response on the conduct that is actually alleged. Both are equally compatible with the principle of not prejudging the outcome. Only the second is compatible with the hearing rule.

The principle in *Dimovski v Howe and Co* adds a dimension that is frequently overlooked: the respondent must have the opportunity to directly address the case against them, not a filtered summary of it. Relying on second-hand accounts and failing to let the employee address the substance of the allegations directly was found to deny the hearing rule's fundamental requirement. The respondent is entitled to know what the evidence shows and to respond to that evidence, not to respond to the investigator's interpretation of it.

A further failure mode warrants specific attention here: the allegation that is treated as unresolvable because the accounts conflict. The investigation that records unable to be substantiated not because the evidence has been assessed but because one person said it happened and one said it did not has not applied the hearing rule. It has avoided applying it. The Commission addressed this directly in *Courtney Sewell v dnata Airport Services Pty Limited* [2025] FWC 2823, finding that allegations can be substantiated on the balance of probabilities even where accounts conflict, if the evidence as a whole supports the finding. The misalignment of accounts is evidence to be assessed. It is not a procedural escape route.

Particularisation does not mean disclosing every piece of evidence gathered. It means stating the allegation with enough detail that the respondent knows what conduct is alleged, when and where it occurred, and what standard it is alleged to breach. The adverse material the investigator intends to rely upon must be disclosed to the respondent before the finding is made. This is not a litigation discovery obligation. It is a procedural fairness obligation, and conflating the two produces either excessive disclosure or insufficient disclosure with equal frequency.

A Genuine Opportunity to Respond

Particularising the allegation is the precondition. Providing a genuine opportunity to respond is the obligation.

The Commission has been consistent about what genuine requires. In *Roy Smout v BHP Coal Pty Ltd*, Commissioner Riordan found that a 5 to 10 minute verbal notification meeting followed by a 30-minute break and then dismissal did not provide a full opportunity to respond. The plain meaning of full: abundant, copious, satisfactory, complete. What that required in practice was the timeframe BHP's own process specified for show cause responses: seven days. The Easter long weekend and the mine divestment deadline were not adequate justifications for compressing that timeframe. Union officials and HR staff are sometimes required to work outside normal hours. The convenience of the employer does not override the respondent's right to a genuine process.

A genuine opportunity to respond is one that allows the respondent to understand the allegation, reflect on it, seek advice from a support person or union official, research their own recollection and any relevant documents, and prepare a considered response. A process that denies any of these elements on grounds of organisational convenience has not provided a genuine opportunity regardless of whether it has provided an opportunity in form.

Section 387(d) of the Fair Work Act establishes that unreasonable refusal to allow a support person at discussions relating to potential dismissal is a factor the Commission must consider when assessing harshness. The right is to the assistance of a person of the respondent's choice, not to legal representation. Its value depends on whether the respondent has had enough time to take instructions from that person before responding. A support person present at a 30-minute meeting at which the termination letter has already been prepared provides no practical assistance, and the Commission found exactly that in *Smout*. The right must be real as well as formal.

When a support person is present, their attendance and identity must be recorded in the investigation record. This is a practical requirement that serves the organisation's defensibility when the process is later reviewed.

The *Ryan v Logan and Co* principle adds a dimension practitioners need to recognise before a show cause meeting is scheduled: a process in which the termination letter has already been drafted, the script has been written, and the decision has in substance already been made is not a show cause process. It is the performance of one. The Commission has found that going through the motions of providing an opportunity to respond when the decision has been made in advance is not compliance with the procedural fairness obligation. The process must be genuine in fact, not just in form. Providing it genuinely, in the timeframe the respondent needs to engage with it, is both the legal requirement and the only version that serves the investigation's integrity.

The Bias Rule in Practice

The legal test for bias in a workplace investigation is not whether the investigator was actually partial. It is whether a fair-minded and informed observer, knowing the circumstances, would reasonably apprehend that the decision-maker might not bring an impartial mind to the question. That is an external standard, applied objectively, and it is considerably harder to satisfy than a subjective belief in one's own fairness.

In *Roy Smout v BHP Coal Pty Ltd*, Commissioner Riordan found that the investigator, a Senior Associate from Minter Ellison with more than 100 investigations of experience, was neither external nor independent. The investigator had shared draft findings with BHP senior staff before finalising the report. He had conducted the complainant interviews by telephone while conducting the respondent interview by video. He had asked leading questions rather than open probing ones. He had failed to identify and interview a witness who had been described by both complainants. The Commission's finding was precise: a proportion of the report was flawed, and the investigation had not been conducted with the independent rigour an external process requires.

Independence is not established by credentials or contractual status. It is demonstrated by method.

The practical bias obligations for investigators are specific. The investigator must not discuss preliminary findings or impressions with the decision-maker or anyone else with a stake in the outcome before the investigation is complete. They must not ask leading questions designed to confirm a view already formed. They must identify and interview witnesses whose evidence may support or contradict any account, not only those whose evidence is consistent with the primary narrative. They must produce a report recording the evidence, the reasoning, and the basis for each finding so that any reviewer can assess the quality of the reasoning rather than accept the conclusion.

The most common form of apprehended bias in workplace investigations is not hostility to the respondent. It is the investigator who has received a substantive briefing from the person who commissioned the investigation and absorbed, perhaps without awareness, the frame that briefing established. Power shapes process before a single question is asked. The senior leader whose account of events is treated as background context rather than as evidence to be tested. The investigator who adjusts their findings in response to client feedback before the report is finalised. A fair-minded observer of either of those circumstances would have grounds to question the impartiality of the process.

The structural dimension of bias is the variant of this problem that practitioners in smaller organisations encounter most acutely. Where the investigator, the relevant manager, the decision-maker, and the parties are all known to each other, and where the political dynamics of the organisation produce additional pressure that has no equivalent in larger employers, the apparent-impartiality threshold the bias rule applies is harder to satisfy from inside the organisation than the practitioner's good faith alone can answer for. The handbook's response is structural rather than personal: where the available investigator cannot satisfy the fair-minded observer test, the appropriate course is to engage external investigation rather than to proceed and rely on the practitioner's belief in their own impartiality. The bias rule does not test belief. It tests appearance, and appearance in a small organisation is shaped by relationships and history that the external standard does not pause for.

This is also the point at which the natural justice framework does something for the investigator that is rarely named directly. The investigator who is being pressed by a senior leader to produce a particular finding is under a specific form of pressure that is difficult to resist as a matter of personal courage alone. The standard, applied externally, becomes the answer to that pressure. The Burchell Test, the hearing rule, the bias rule, the apprehended bias standard: these are not only protections for the parties. They are the external scaffolding that allows the investigator to say, in response to pressure for a predetermined outcome, that the process cannot be conducted as requested without producing a finding that the Commission would set aside.

The Stop Bullying Benchbook adds a dimension that closes the logical loop on why the bias rule matters beyond procedural compliance. An investigation conducted in a manner that is grossly unfair is itself a form of unreasonable conduct that can constitute workplace bullying. The investigator who weaponises the process, who conducts it with malicious intent or contempt for the respondent's dignity, has not only produced a finding that will not survive scrutiny. They have created new liability for the organisation that commissioned the investigation. Natural justice is not just the standard the investigation must meet. It is the protection against the investigation itself becoming the harm.

Post-Investigation Procedural Obligations

Natural justice does not end when the investigation report is finalised. It continues through the decision-making stage, and failures at this stage are at least as common as failures during the investigation itself.

The decision-maker who receives a finding of serious misconduct and proceeds directly to dismissal without a show cause process has not provided the procedural fairness the Fair Work Act requires. The investigator's finding is not the dismissal. The dismissal is a separate decision, made by a separate person, following a separate process that must include notification of the proposed action, an opportunity for the respondent to respond to that proposed action, and genuine consideration of that response before the decision is finalised. These obligations are additional to the opportunity to respond to investigation findings. They are not the same obligation expressed twice.

The complainant's post-investigation entitlements are equally specific and equally frequently neglected. *Courtney Sewell v dnata Airport Services Pty Limited* [2025] FWC 2823 makes the standard concrete. The investigation found the sexual harassment allegations unsubstantiated. The verbal outcome was communicated to the complainant, but the written outcome letter did not follow for weeks and only after she requested it. When it arrived, the letter described the findings as unable to make a finding for some of the allegations, language so ambiguous she could not determine what had been found. Her request to be rostered away from the alleged harasser was refused. No workable return-to-work arrangement was provided. The Commission found constructive dismissal and awarded $36,468.39 in compensation. The investigation itself was not the failure. What followed it was.

The obligation to advise the complainant of the outcome is a procedural fairness requirement reflecting the complainant's legitimate interest in knowing their complaint was taken seriously, and their right to be treated with dignity throughout a process they initiated at personal risk. The communication must be clear enough to be understood, timely enough to be useful, and specific enough to tell the complainant what was found without disclosing material that the respondent's privacy right protects.

Both parties are owed an explanation of the outcome, in clear terms, in writing, within a timeframe that serves their legitimate interest in knowing what the process produced. The structure of that communication, the timing, and the management of the return-to-work or disciplinary action that follows, is the subject of Chapter Ten. The procedural fairness principle is established here. The decision-maker who treats the investigation report as the end of the process rather than as the beginning of the next one has misunderstood where their own procedural obligations sit.

Procedural Fairness as a Positive Duty

The formulation of procedural fairness as a constraint, a set of requirements the investigator must satisfy to avoid a finding of unfairness, is accurate but insufficient.

The more complete formulation is this: procedural fairness is the structure through which people can trust a process that will affect them. That trust is not an incidental benefit. It is the mechanism through which the investigation produces its most important outputs: testimony from people who feel safe enough to give it accurately, genuine engagement from a respondent who understands they will be heard, and findings that a decision-maker can act upon with confidence.

The psychosocial hazard code of practice identifies poor organisational justice as a registered psychosocial hazard with three operational dimensions: procedural justice through fair processes, informational fairness through keeping people appropriately informed, and interpersonal fairness through treating people with dignity and respect throughout. When workers perceive a process as unfair, the health consequences include anxiety, depression, post-traumatic stress disorder, and the chronic physical conditions associated with prolonged stress. These consequences do not wait for a wrong finding. They follow from a process conducted in a way that denies people the dignity and information they are owed, regardless of the outcome.

Employers carry a positive duty to prevent these harms, not merely to respond to them. That duty runs through the investigation from intake to outcome communication. The investigator who understands natural justice only as a compliance obligation will satisfy it at the minimum level the scrutiny requires. The investigator who understands it as the structure through which the investigation's integrity is maintained will apply it because the investigation demands it.

PRACTITIONER NOTE

The procedural failure most likely to be present in an investigation that feels fair is the allegation that does not say enough.

The practitioner who sends a notification letter describing allegations of inappropriate behaviour in the workplace has not notified the respondent of the allegation. They have notified them that an allegation exists. The respondent who receives that letter cannot assess it against their own recollection because they do not know what conduct is alleged. They cannot identify relevant witnesses because they do not know what incident is in question. They cannot prepare a considered response because they do not know what they are responding to.

This failure is almost always unintentional. The investigator writes a vague notification because they are trying not to prejudge the outcome, or because the complaint itself is vague and they have not yet done the work of reducing it to specific allegations. Both reasons are understandable. Neither produces a notification that satisfies the hearing rule. The discipline required is to particularise before notifying. If the complaint as received is too vague to allow specific allegations to be drafted, that is a finding about the complaint that needs to be resolved in the preliminary assessment stage, not after notification has been sent.

The second failure pattern is the show cause process that has concluded before it begins. The decision is made. The letter is drafted. The meeting is scheduled. The respondent is given thirty minutes and then dismissed. The Commission, as Smout demonstrates, recognises this pattern precisely: it is not procedural fairness, it is the performance of it, and the performance no longer fools anyone who reads the transcript.

Record whether a support person was present at every meeting related to the investigation or proposed disciplinary action, who they were, and what role they played. That record protects the process when its adequacy is later contested.

A NOTE ON COGNITIVE STYLE

Natural justice produces two specific challenges for practitioners who think in non-linear patterns.

The first is the particularisation stage. Drafting specific allegations requires holding the complaint in a structured analytical frame: what precisely is alleged, when, where, and by reference to what standard. For practitioners who process information holistically and arrive at a complete picture quickly, the discipline of translating that picture into written allegations that can stand alone is effortful. The picture in the practitioner's mind may be accurate. The allegations on the page must be accurate and self-contained, because it is the allegations on the page that the respondent will respond to.

The asset at this stage is the same pattern-recognition capacity that makes the picture form quickly. A non-linear thinker who has formed a complete picture of the alleged conduct is well-placed to identify what specific details are needed to make the allegation particularise. They can see the gaps before they write the letter. The discipline is to use that capacity to check the particularisation rather than assume it.

The second challenge is the bias check. The practitioner who has formed an early view of the case, often a correct view, must apply the fair-minded lay observer test to their own process before the respondent interview is conducted. Has the process, from the outside, the appearance of impartiality? Have the open questions been asked, or the questions that confirm what is already believed? Have witnesses whose evidence might complicate the primary narrative been identified and interviewed? A natural justice checklist held as a standing document in the investigation file is the external prompt that asks these questions at the moment when the pressure to move forward is highest. It does not substitute for judgment. It ensures the judgment has been applied.

What Comes Next

The Terms of Reference are defined. Natural justice and procedural fairness obligations are established and built into the investigation's structure. Both parties have been notified and the process has a legal foundation that can be demonstrated.

Chapter Four addresses the investigation plan: the working document that translates the Terms of Reference into a sequenced, evidence-gathering process with defined decision points, a clear timeline, and the mechanisms for managing the investigation's integrity as evidence develops. Planning is where the investigative standard becomes operational. The quality of the plan determines the quality of everything that follows.

Chapter Four

Planning the Investigation

An unplanned investigation is not a flexible one. It is an investigation that will have to be partially repeated.

The practitioner who begins interviewing before the evidence has been mapped, who sequences witnesses by availability rather than strategy, who has not decided what documentary evidence to seek before the first interview takes place, is not conducting an open and responsive inquiry. They are accumulating material that may or may not answer the question the Terms of Reference have defined, in an order that may or may not preserve the reliability of what they find. When the finding is challenged, the absence of a plan is not evidence of flexibility. It is evidence that the process was not designed to produce a defensible outcome.

The investigation you rushed today is the Fair Work Commission reversal you will explain in six months.

The investigation plan is the document that translates the Terms of Reference into an operational sequence. It is not a bureaucratic requirement. It is the investigation's working logic, held in a form that can be consulted, revised, and if necessary defended. A practitioner who has a plan knows what they are doing and why. A practitioner who does not is making those decisions under the pressure of the investigation itself, at exactly the moments when that pressure is most likely to distort them.

The counterargument is that planning takes time that urgent matters cannot afford. The answer is that the time a plan saves in the investigation's middle and closing stages is always greater than the time it costs at the start. The investigation that has to be partially repeated because witnesses were interviewed in an order that allowed evidence contamination, or because documentary evidence was sought after interviews rather than before, does not save time by skipping the plan. It loses time compoundingly, and it loses it at the stage when the investigation is already under scrutiny.

What the Plan Must Cover

An investigation plan is a working document. It will be revised as the investigation develops. Its value is not that it predicts every development but that it establishes the investigation's decision-making framework before the pressure to make decisions in real time has arrived.

A complete investigation plan covers seven elements. Each element has a concrete output the plan must record.

1. The allegations and the evidence required to address them

Each allegation in the Terms of Reference is mapped against the categories of evidence that would be relevant to it. Not every piece of evidence that might conceivably exist, but the evidence that would, if it exists, bear on whether the allegation is supported on the balance of probabilities. This mapping exercise produces two outputs simultaneously: a written list of evidence to be sought, and a preliminary identification of the gaps that would represent the alternative explanation in the absence of that evidence. Both outputs feed directly into the evidence matrix described later in this chapter.

2. The interview sequence

Who will be interviewed, in what order, and why. This is the element most often left to availability rather than strategy, and it is where strategic thinking produces the most direct benefits. The general principle is that documentary evidence is secured before interviews begin wherever possible, witnesses are interviewed before principals, and the respondent is interviewed after the complainant and relevant witnesses. The reasoning in each case is the same: the interview sequence should be designed to preserve the independence of each account rather than allow earlier accounts to shape later ones. Where any party is known or appears to be neurodivergent, the plan should include an accommodation assessment at this stage: what adjustments to format, timing, communication method, or support may be required to ensure that party can participate in the process on equal terms. The output is a written interview schedule with the reasoning for the sequence recorded next to it.

3. The documentary evidence to be sought

What records exist, where they are held, who controls access to them, and in what format they need to be obtained to be useful. This includes electronic records, CCTV, access logs, timesheets, payroll records, performance documentation, emails and messaging platform records, and any other records whose existence can be anticipated from the nature of the allegations. The plan specifies the mechanism for requesting these records and the timeline for receiving them before the relevant interviews take place. The output is a categorised evidence request schedule with preservation requests made before collection begins. The detailed mechanics of evidence collection are addressed in Chapter Five.

4. The timeline

When each step of the investigation will be completed, what the expected completion date is, who has oversight and how they will be updated, and what the decision criteria are for extending the timeline if circumstances require it. The timeline is not a commitment to a specific outcome date. It is a working framework that identifies when the investigation is running behind and why, so that extensions can be managed transparently. It must also address informational fairness: both parties are entitled to know the expected timeframe for the investigation and to be updated if that timeframe changes. Keeping people informed about matters that affect them is a pillar of organisational justice, and leaving parties in silence about progress is a procedural failure independent of what the investigation eventually finds. The output is a dated timeline with named decision points and update obligations.

5. The oversight and conflict management framework

Who commissioned the investigation, who the investigator reports to, who the decision-maker will be, and how conflicts of interest will be identified and managed if they arise. This element is the one most likely to be assumed rather than documented, and the assumption is most likely to be wrong in the cases where it matters most. The output is a written reporting and decision-maker structure naming each role and the conflict management protocol.

6. The investigation log

Not a section of the plan itself, but a companion document that the plan establishes and the investigator opens at the planning stage. The investigation log is the real-time record of every decision made during the investigation, the evidence considered in making it, and the reasoning that supported it. Its primary function is not compliance. It is cognitive: an investigation that generates a complex and shifting evidence base produces a large number of small decisions whose rationale degrades quickly in memory. The log is the record of why things were done in the order they were done, which is the information a reviewer needs when assessing whether the process was reasonable. Critically, the log must record not only the evidence sought and found but the evidence not pursued and the reason why. If a category of potentially relevant evidence was not sought, that decision must be documented. An unrecorded non-pursuit is not a considered judgment. It is a gap. The output is an open log document with the first entries made at the planning stage.

7. The concurrent WHS assessment

The investigation plan must include an explicit determination of whether a concurrent Work Health and Safety investigation is required. A disciplinary investigation and a WHS investigation serve different purposes and must be conducted separately. The disciplinary investigation addresses whether specific conduct breached a standard. The WHS investigation addresses whether the workplace conditions that gave rise to the complaint represent an ongoing psychosocial hazard that must be controlled regardless of the disciplinary outcome. The employer's primary duty of care under s.19 of the Work Health and Safety Act 2011 requires the identification and control of psychosocial risks. That duty does not pause during a disciplinary investigation, and a finding that the alleged conduct was unsubstantiated does not discharge it. The output is a recorded assessment of whether a concurrent WHS inquiry is being conducted and, if one is not, why.

The Interview Sequence

The decision about who to interview first, and in what order, is the planning decision with the most direct consequences for the reliability of the evidence produced.

The principle is straightforward: each witness should provide their account independently, before they know what others have said. The practice is more complex, because in most workplace investigations the parties already know each other, already know that a complaint has been made, and have often already discussed the events in question before the investigation begins.

The contamination risk is real and it is not always deliberate. A witness who has discussed the events with the complainant before being interviewed is not necessarily tailoring their account to support the complaint. They may have incorporated elements of the complainant's account into their own memory of what they observed, a process cognitive psychology identifies as source monitoring error: the failure to distinguish between what was directly experienced and what was later learned. The interview that follows will not detect this error because the witness genuinely believes their account is their own recollection.

A further mechanism compounds this risk. Research on social proof shows that people determine what is correct partly by observing what others believe is correct. A witness who has heard the complainant's account does not need to decide consciously to align with it. The alignment may occur through the natural process of constructing a coherent understanding of an event from multiple inputs, in which the most recently heard account carries disproportionate weight. The investigator who assumes the accounts were aligned through collusion may be wrong. The investigator who assumes they were not affected by contact between the parties is more likely to be wrong.

The sequencing strategy that minimises this risk follows a consistent logic. Documents before any interviews. Witnesses before principals. Complainant before respondent, so the respondent can respond to the complete account. Where multiple witnesses exist, an assessment of which are least likely to have been in contact with each other, interviewed first. And where a witness is neurodivergent or requires accommodation, the sequencing plan must build in the additional preparation and support time needed.

The simultaneous notification problem deserves attention. When parties are notified of the investigation at the same time, the period between notification and interview is a window in which accounts can be aligned. This is not a reason to delay notification. It is a reason to sequence interviews as quickly as possible after notification and to include in the notification a clear statement that parties should not discuss the investigation with colleagues who may be called as witnesses. That instruction cannot be enforced in the same way a court can enforce a suppression order. Its inclusion establishes that the organisation took the contamination risk seriously, which is relevant if account alignment is raised later.

Securing Documentary Evidence at the Planning Stage

Documentary evidence should be secured before the interview phase begins wherever the nature of the investigation allows it. This is the default position from which departures should be deliberate rather than inadvertent. The detailed methods for collecting, handling, and authenticating documentary evidence are the subject of Chapter Five. The planning-stage focus is preservation and sequencing.

The reasons for sequencing documents before interviews are practical. A witness interviewed before their own records have been reviewed is a missed opportunity: the investigator does not yet know what the records show and cannot ask the questions the records make possible. An interview conducted after the records are available allows the investigator to probe inconsistencies between account and documentary evidence, which is among the most reliable sources of credibility assessment available.

The urgency of preservation is distinct from the process of collection and must be addressed as a separate step at the planning stage. Email records, CCTV footage, access logs, and voicemails can be overwritten, deleted, or archived on automated cycles that do not pause for investigations. The investigator who plans to collect these records next week may find they no longer exist. Preservation requests must be made at the planning stage, before collection begins, to ensure the records are held in their current state until they can be properly retrieved and assessed. The standard preservation request identifies the categories of records to be preserved, the relevant date range, the systems on which they are likely to be held, and the instruction not to overwrite, delete, or archive them until the investigator confirms in writing that the preservation hold can be lifted.

The categories of documentary evidence relevant to most workplace investigations include: employment records, rosters and access logs establishing who was where and when; email and messaging records documenting communications between parties and witnesses; CCTV and physical access records where the alleged conduct occurred in a monitored location; performance records and prior complaints establishing relevant context; and contemporaneous records created by the parties themselves, including diary entries, notes, and messages to third parties in the period immediately following the alleged conduct. The plan should identify which of these categories are likely to be relevant and which preservation requests are needed for each.

Contemporaneous records are among the most valuable evidence available in workplace investigations and among the most frequently overlooked. A complainant who messaged a friend after an incident describing what happened has produced a record of their immediate response that is harder to retrospectively construct than testimony given weeks later. The investigator who does not ask for this type of evidence at the planning stage has not asked one of the most important questions available.

In *Roy Smout v BHP Coal Pty Ltd* [2024] FWC 2062, the Commission's criticism included the failure to use attendance records and security photographs to identify a witness who had been described by both complainants. The documentary equivalent of an unrecorded non-pursuit is the evidence that could have been retrieved but was not sought, and was not sought without a recorded reason. The plan is the document that prevents that failure by requiring those decisions to be made deliberately at the outset.

The Evidence Matrix

The evidence matrix is the planning tool that holds the evidential state of the investigation in a visible, navigable form. It is a working tool, not a compliance document.

The structure is straightforward. Each allegation in the Terms of Reference occupies a row. The elements of that allegation occupy sub-rows. Each column represents a category of evidence: complainant account, respondent account, witness one, witness two, documentary evidence, contemporaneous records, and any other category the investigation requires. The cells record what evidence exists, what it shows, and whether it supports or contradicts the element it relates to. A practitioner can build this in a spreadsheet in fifteen minutes. The discipline of maintaining it produces benefits across the rest of the investigation that no other single tool replicates.

The matrix serves three functions simultaneously. It makes evidentiary gaps visible before the investigation closes: the empty cell is a question the investigation has not yet answered, and the decision about whether that question must be answered before a finding can be reached should be made deliberately. It maps the alternative explanation: the pattern of evidence that supports a finding also reveals, by contrast, what evidence would be required to support the alternative, and whether that pattern is present. And it provides the structural foundation for the investigation report: the report's findings should be traceable to the matrix without inconsistency.

In investigations where the primary evidence is testimonial and the accounts conflict, the evidence matrix must include a column for rationally probative material beyond direct corroboration: the complainant's emotional state and behaviour immediately following the alleged incident, the timing and content of any disclosure to a third party, any prior similar conduct by the respondent, and any physical or environmental evidence that supports or contradicts the account's plausibility. Treating conflicting accounts as automatically unresolvable and recording a finding of unsubstantiated without assessing this material is not a planning failure. It is an evidentiary failure, and it begins at the planning stage when the matrix does not include the columns that would have prompted the assessment.

For investigations involving multiple allegations and multiple parties, the evidence matrix is the document that prevents the investigation from becoming unmanageable. The investigator tracking the evidential state of eight allegations across twelve witnesses and forty documents in working memory alone is operating beyond what working memory can reliably sustain under sustained pressure. The matrix externalises that load so cognitive capacity can be directed at assessment rather than inventory.

The Investigation Log

The investigation log is the real-time record of the investigation's decision-making. It is distinct from the evidence matrix and distinct from the investigation report. Its purpose is to document why decisions were made, not what evidence was found.

Every decision of substance made during the investigation should be recorded: the decision to include or exclude a witness, the decision to seek or not seek a category of documentary evidence, the decision to expand or contract scope in response to something that emerged during an interview, the decision to extend the timeline and the reason for it. Each entry should record the date, the decision, the evidence or reasoning that supported it, and the alternative that was considered and rejected.

The non-pursuit record deserves separate emphasis. The decision not to interview a witness is only a decision if it has been made deliberately. If a witness never appeared on the interview list because no one thought of them, that is not a decision. It is a gap. The log, maintained from the planning stage, converts defaults into recorded judgments. If a category of potentially relevant evidence was not pursued, the reason must be documented. Under the Burchell Test, the reasonableness of an investigation is assessed against the decisions made and the grounds for making them. An investigation log that contains only the evidence gathered provides half the record. The other half is the evidence not pursued, and why.

The log's value at the planning stage is that it forces the investigator to make explicit the decisions that would otherwise be made by default. It also serves as the re-entry tool when an investigation is interrupted. An investigation paused while awaiting documentary evidence or a witness's availability must be re-entered with full context intact. The practitioner who returns to the log can reconstruct exactly where the investigation stands without holding the full evidential state in memory across the interruption.

Proportionality in Planning

The investigation plan should include a proportionality assessment made at the outset and revisited if the scope changes.

Proportionality is the alignment between the complexity and seriousness of the allegations and the resources, time, and process applied to address them. An investigation that is too thin for the allegations produces findings that will not survive scrutiny. An investigation that is more extensive than the allegations warrant causes harm to all parties that is not justified by the findings it is capable of producing. The employer's primary duty of care under the WHS Act includes the obligation to ensure, as far as is reasonably practicable, that the investigation process itself does not create or amplify psychosocial harm. An investigation that is disproportionately burdensome is not more rigorous. It is more harmful, and the harm falls on the people who have to live through it.

The proportionality assessment addresses three questions. Does the formal investigation process match the nature and seriousness of the allegations? Is the scope the minimum necessary to answer the question the Terms of Reference have defined? And is the timeline proportionate to what the investigation actually requires, or has it been set to the organisation's administrative convenience rather than the investigation's genuine needs?

Proportionality also has an organisational dimension that practitioners in small businesses, council HR teams, and resource-constrained agencies must address directly. The methodology described in this handbook scales to the resources available without abandoning its standards, but the elements that scale and the elements that do not must be distinguished. The non-negotiable elements are the ones that protect the parties' procedural rights and the investigation's evidentiary integrity: particularised allegations notified to the respondent, a genuine opportunity to respond, witnesses interviewed in a sequence that minimises contamination, a reasoned finding made by reference to the evidence and the alternative explanation, a finding communicated to both parties in clear terms, and a safety assessment that addresses the workplace conditions independently of the disciplinary finding. None of these requires significant resources to apply. They require deliberate application of a discipline that the resource-constrained practitioner is fully capable of. The elements that scale with resources are the ones that make a complex investigation easier to manage but that are not strictly required by the standard: dedicated case management software, parallel investigation teams, external legal advice on each procedural question. A spreadsheet applied consistently will produce a defensible evidence matrix. A single practitioner working to a structured plan will reach a defensible finding. The discipline required is greater than the resources required.

Managing the Investigation Under Pressure

The investigation plan does not eliminate the pressure that investigations generate. It provides a framework within which that pressure can be managed without distorting the process.

The most common forms of investigative pressure are organisational, temporal, and relational. Organisational pressure arrives when the person who commissioned the investigation has a preferred outcome and is not subtle about it. Temporal pressure arrives when external deadlines are creating urgency that the investigation cannot absorb without compromising its integrity. Relational pressure arrives when the investigator has a relationship with one or more parties that makes impartial application of the process uncomfortable.

The investigation plan addresses all three forms of pressure in the same way: by establishing the decision-making framework before the pressure arrives, so that departures from it are recognisable rather than invisible. An investigator who has a plan knows when they are being asked to depart from it. An investigator who has an investigation log knows when a decision was made under pressure that would not have been made otherwise. The plan and the log together produce a record that supports the investigator's professional judgment when that judgment is questioned by people whose preferred outcome was not what the evidence supported.

The failure in *Smout v BHP* was not that BHP faced a deadline. It was that the deadline was allowed to determine the investigation's quality rather than its timeline. Two and a half weeks of inaction followed by a seven-day investigation conducted under the pressure of an Easter long weekend and a mine divestment was not a reasonable investigation under the Burchell Test. The plan, established at the outset with a realistic timeline, would have made the gap between the organisation's administrative needs and the investigation's requirements visible before it became a Fair Work Commission finding. Instead, the gap was invisible until it was not.

PRACTITIONER NOTE

An investigator who sequences witnesses by their availability is not conducting an inquiry. They are allowing the respondents' calendars to design the finding.

This is the planning failure most likely to be invisible until it matters. In most cases the sequence by availability produces no consequence. In the case where a key witness discusses their account with the complainant between notification and interview, it produces a consequence the investigation cannot recover from. The witness will not know their account has been affected. The investigator will not be able to see it. The finding will reflect it in ways that may not become apparent until the evidence is tested at hearing.

The sequencing decision takes ten minutes to make deliberately. Explaining why the sequence turned out to have mattered takes considerably longer.

The second failure is the evidence not sought without a recorded reason. The decision not to interview a witness, not to retrieve a category of documents, not to seek a contemporaneous record that the complainant mentioned in passing: each of these is a decision that must be recorded, with the reasoning that supported it. If the reasoning was we did not think of it, that is not a recorded decision. It is a gap that becomes visible only when someone with a strong interest in the process's failure identifies it.

The third failure is the preservation gap. The plan includes documentary evidence to be sought. It must also include the preservation requests made before collection begins. CCTV footage overwritten on a standard cycle. Email records archived before the retrieval request arrives. Access logs purged at the end of the month. These are not failures of investigation. They are failures of planning, and the evidence lost is lost permanently.

A NOTE ON COGNITIVE STYLE

The investigation plan is the document that does the most work for practitioners whose cognitive strengths include non-linear connection-making and whose challenges include sequential task management under competing demands.

An investigation without a plan presents as an open field of relevant considerations, all visible simultaneously and none with a defined relationship to the others. For a practitioner whose mind generates connections across the full field, this is not clarifying. It is overwhelming. The plan does not reduce the field. It sequences it, which is a different and more useful function: the full field remains visible, but the question of what to do next has an answer.

The evidence matrix serves a related function for practitioners who generate hypotheses quickly. The pattern-recognition capacity that allows a non-linear thinker to see the shape of the allegation before the evidence is fully gathered is an asset at assessment and a liability at planning if it is allowed to determine the sequence before the evidence has been tested. The matrix makes the hypothesis explicit and visible, which means it can be tested rather than assumed.

The investigation log is the re-entry tool for a complex investigation that has been interrupted. An investigation paused for a week while a key witness is unavailable, or while a documentary evidence request is being processed, must be re-entered with full context intact. The practitioner who returns to the log can reconstruct exactly where the investigation stands and why, without holding the full evidential state in memory across the interruption. For investigations of any complexity, this is not a minor convenience. It is the difference between a managed pause and a missed step.

What Comes Next

The investigation has a plan. The evidence matrix is established. The interview sequence is set. The documentary evidence preservation requests have been made and the collection process has begun. The investigation log is open.

Chapter Five addresses the gathering of evidence: the principles and methods for collecting documentary, physical, and testimonial evidence in a way that preserves its reliability and its defensibility. Evidence gathering is where the plan meets the reality of what is actually available, and the gap between those two things is where the investigator's judgment is most directly tested.

Chapter Five

Gathering Evidence

The evidence base you planned will be wrong.

Not entirely wrong. The plan gives you the starting map: the allegations, the likely records, the probable witnesses. But the map is drawn before the territory has been explored, and the territory of a workplace investigation never matches the map exactly. A document that was not anticipated turns out to be central. A witness whose account was expected to confirm the primary account has observed something no one else did. The gathering phase is the first encounter between the investigation's working hypothesis and the reality of what the evidence base actually contains.

The practitioner who treats evidence gathering as the execution of a predetermined checklist produces an evidence base that reflects the assumptions built into the plan. The practitioner who treats it as an open inquiry, following what the evidence suggests rather than only what was anticipated, produces an evidence base capable of supporting a defensible finding. The distinction between these two approaches is the difference between an investigation that confirms and an investigation that tests.

The Hierarchy of Evidence

Documentary evidence is the primary anchor of investigative reliability.

Documents produced before the investigation began, without knowledge of how they would be used, are not affected by the motivated reasoning that shapes retrospective testimony. This is not a claim that documents are infallible. They may contain errors, missing values, or inconsistent entries that require assessment. Documents created by parties with an interest in the outcome require the same scrutiny as testimony from those parties. The hierarchy is about susceptibility to the processes that most commonly undermine reliability in workplace investigations, and documents produced before the complaint was made are less susceptible to those processes than accounts provided after the investigation has begun.

Within testimonial evidence, contemporaneous accounts are more reliable than retrospective ones. A witness who disclosed the incident to a colleague the same day it occurred, whose message record contains that disclosure, has produced evidence of their immediate response that is independent of anything they say in an interview weeks later. That contemporaneous record is not just corroboration of their account. It is evidence of the emotional and cognitive state in which they reported it, which is relevant to the assessment of reliability independent of whether their later account is internally consistent.

This hierarchy has a specific practical implication that the investigator must not miss: the absence of documentary corroboration does not permit a default finding of unsubstantiated. The Fair Work Commission addressed this directly in *Courtney Sewell v dnata Airport Services Pty Limited* [2025] FWC 2823, finding that an investigation was fatally flawed by the assumption that where evidence was misaligned, meaning one person's account contradicted another's, the allegation was automatically unable to be substantiated. Allegations can be substantiated on the balance of probabilities even where no independent witness exists and no document directly records the conduct, if the evidence as a whole, including the complainant's immediate disclosure and emotional state, supports the finding. The absence of a corroborating document is evidence to be weighed. It is not a reason to stop weighing.

The target standard for the evidence base is the balance of probabilities: is the existence of each relevant fact more probable than not? Every gathering decision, what to seek, what to retrieve, what to assess, is calibrated against this standard. Evidence that has no bearing on whether any relevant fact is more probable than not does not need to be gathered. Evidence that does bear on that question must be sought unless there is a recorded reason why seeking it is disproportionate to its likely value.

Collecting Documentary Evidence

Documentary evidence collection requires three things: identification, preservation, and authentication.

Identification is the process of establishing what records exist that are relevant to the allegations. The evidence map produced in the planning phase gives the starting point. The investigation itself will reveal additional records as the inquiry develops. The investigator should approach identification with two questions asked simultaneously: if this allegation is true, what records would that have generated? And its inverse: if it is not true, what records would demonstrate that? Both questions produce different evidence searches. Running both simultaneously is the alternative hypothesis test applied to documentary evidence.

Preservation must be addressed before collection. Email records, CCTV footage, access logs, and voicemails can be overwritten, deleted, or archived on automated cycles. Preservation requests must be made at the planning stage to ensure records are held in their current state until they can be properly retrieved and assessed. Chapter Four covered the preservation request mechanics. The relevant principle at the collection stage is simply that preservation precedes retrieval, and a retrieval attempt that finds the record no longer exists is not a collection failure. It is a planning failure made visible at the collection stage.

Authentication is the process of establishing that a document is what it appears to be. Five questions determine whether a record can be relied upon. Where did the record originate? Why was it created? How has it been stored and who has had access to it? What personal information does it contain and what obligations govern its handling? In what form is it being used in the investigation? These questions are not bureaucratic checkboxes. They are the framework for assessing whether a record can be relied upon or whether its reliability is itself in question. A record whose provenance cannot be established, whose creation purpose is unclear, whose storage history includes unaccounted-for access, or whose form in the investigation is different from its original form, all require a specific assessment of weight before being included in the matrix.

Transparency with all parties about how personal information will be handled is an obligation, not a courtesy. The HRPA Practice Standard is specific: investigators must be transparent about how privacy and confidentiality will be preserved and must not give absolute guarantees of confidentiality. A witness who has been told their account will be kept strictly confidential, when it may be disclosed to the respondent as adverse material, has been misled. That misrepresentation may affect their willingness to participate in subsequent proceedings and creates a procedural vulnerability that the investigation itself created.

The Privacy Act 1988 (Cth) governs personal information collected during investigations. The Employee Record Exemption means private sector employers are generally exempt from the Act's obligations in relation to employee records used for employment-related purposes. Collection must nonetheless be proportionate to the investigation's scope. Records collected for the investigation must be stored securely, accessed only by those with a legitimate need, and not disclosed beyond the purposes for which they were gathered. For public sector practitioners in Victoria, the Charter of Human Rights and Responsibilities Act 2006 s.13 adds a specific obligation: collection of personal information must not constitute unlawful or arbitrary interference with privacy, which means collection must be no broader than the investigation requires.

Email and Messaging Evidence

An investigator who relies on the complainant's screenshots is not conducting an inquiry. They are allowing the complainant to curate the truth.

The first problem is platform proliferation. Most workplace communications now occur across multiple channels: employer email systems, messaging platforms, personal messaging applications, and social media. Each has different data retention policies, different access protocols, and different evidentiary implications. The investigator whose evidence plan covers only the employer email system has mapped one channel of a multi-channel communication environment.

The second problem is screenshot evidence. A screenshot provided by a party to the investigation shows what that party chose to capture, in the cropping they chose, at the time they chose to take it. It may omit preceding context that changes the meaning of the captured exchange. It may have been edited. It may represent a selective extract from a longer conversation. Screenshots provided by parties should be assessed as testimonial evidence, not documentary evidence: they are the party's account of what the record shows, and that account requires the same scrutiny as any other testimonial account.

Where employer-controlled systems contain relevant communications, those records should be retrieved independently through the appropriate IT or HR process rather than accepted from the parties. The independently retrieved record has a provenance that can be established. The screenshot does not.

The third problem is deletion and the inference available from it. Where records that would be expected to exist have been deleted or cannot be located, the investigator should document the absence and assess what inference is available. A record deleted after the investigation began is different from a record deleted as part of a routine archiving process that preceded the complaint. The timing and circumstances of deletion are evidence. The absence of an expected record is evidence. The empty cell in the matrix is not neutral.

Edit histories, timestamp metadata, and read receipts are available in many employer-controlled systems and are among the most overlooked categories of evidence in workplace investigations. A message edited after the investigation began, a document accessed by the respondent after the complaint was made, a read receipt showing a policy was opened at a relevant time: these are potentially material evidence requiring no additional testimony to establish and impossible to retrospectively create once the investigation closes. The investigator who does not request this metadata at the time of retrieval may find it permanently unavailable when the relevance becomes apparent.

Physical Evidence and Environmental Assessment

The physical context of alleged conduct is evidence, and it must be assessed while it is available.

The location where alleged conduct occurred may support or undermine accounts of what was possible. In *Roy Smout v BHP Coal Pty Ltd* [2024] FWC 2062, one complainant was operating a loud cleaning machine at the time an alleged comment was made. The investigator did not ask about the noise conditions. Under cross-examination at the Fair Work Commission hearing, the complainant acknowledged she had not heard the comment. An assessment of the environmental conditions, conducted during the evidence-gathering phase, would have identified this before the finding was made rather than after it was challenged.

The principle is not that every investigation requires a site visit. It is that the physical context of alleged conduct should be assessed for its relevance to what could have been seen, heard, or done in that location at that time. CCTV coverage, noise levels, sight lines, access restrictions, and the presence of other people are all potentially relevant. All can be assessed from records or a brief environmental review. Once the investigation closes and the physical environment changes, this evidence cannot be retrospectively recreated.

Witness Evidence and the Limits of Testimony

Human memory is not a recording. It is a reconstruction.

Each time a memory is retrieved, it is partially reconstructed from available traces, and the reconstruction is shaped by everything the person knows and believes at the time of retrieval. Post-event information, including accounts heard from other witnesses, discussions with colleagues, and the questions asked in a previous interview, can alter the memory of the original event without the witness being aware of it. This is not dishonesty. It is the normal operation of human memory under normal conditions, and it is why the conditions under which testimony is obtained matter as much as the testimony itself.

Witnesses should be interviewed as soon as possible after the alleged conduct occurred, before post-event information has shaped their recollection. The interview environment should support accurate retrieval: a witness who is anxious, defensive, or distressed is less able to search their memory accurately. The questions asked should invite narrative rather than confirm a hypothesis. An open question that allows the witness to describe what they experienced produces more reliable evidence than a series of closed questions that confirm or deny specific propositions. Closed questions in an investigative context do not merely collect less reliable evidence. They actively shape the evidence they collect: when a witness in a formal process, with a person of institutional authority asking specific questions, stops retrieving their own memory and starts responding to what the questions suggest, the testimony has become a product of the questioning rather than a product of the recollection. The interviewing methodology that operationalises these principles is the subject of Chapter Six.

A caution applies where a party or witness is neurodivergent. A complainant or witness with a non-linear working memory may produce contemporaneous records that are fragmented, tonally inconsistent, or chronologically out of sequence without those features reflecting dishonesty or unreliability. Interpreting fragmented records as fabricated, or chronological inconsistency as a credibility indicator, is a category error. The content and corroborating context of the record matter. The format in which a neurodivergent person recorded their experience does not.

Witness evidence should be recorded in a form that preserves the account as provided. A verbatim record, or a record that clearly distinguishes between the witness's language and the investigator's, is more defensible than a paraphrase. The paraphrase is the investigator's interpretation of what was said. That interpretation may reflect the investigator's existing view of the case in ways invisible in the record.

Absent and Destroyed Evidence

The absence of expected evidence requires assessment, not notation.

Expected evidence that does not exist falls into categories with different implications. Records that should have been created and were not may indicate a relevant process was not followed. Records created but not locatable may have been misfiled, archived, or deleted, each with different implications that should be investigated before being treated as equivalent. Records deleted after the relevant conduct occurred or after the investigation began carry different evidential weight from records deleted as part of a routine process that preceded both. Records a party claims do not exist, but which circumstantial evidence suggests should, require a specific assessment of whether the explanation for their absence is plausible.

The inference available from absent evidence depends on the circumstances. In some cases the absence is powerful evidence. In others it is neutral. What it is never is invisible: the investigation report must address what was sought and not found, and why, because the record of a complete evidence-gathering process includes a record of what was looked for and not found. An investigation report that addresses only what was gathered implies only what was gathered mattered. That implication will be tested if the finding is challenged.

A practical discipline applies here. When evidence is found to be absent, the investigator should record three things: the evidence expected to exist, the reason it was expected, and the assessment of what its absence means. The third element is the one most likely to be omitted. An investigation log entry reading email records sought, not located is a notation. An entry reading email records sought, not located, IT confirms standard retention period had not expired, no explanation for absence has been provided by the respondent, absence assessed as carrying adverse inference is an assessment. The difference between the two is the difference between a record of activity and a record of reasoning.

Managing Evidence from Multiple Sources

Complex investigations generate evidence from multiple sources that must be held together coherently. The evidence matrix is the tool for this. The discipline of populating it consistently, recording what each piece of evidence shows in relation to each element of each allegation, prevents the investigation from drowning in material it cannot assess.

The specific risk in evidence-rich investigations is the availability heuristic: the tendency to weight evidence that is vivid, recent, and easily recalled more heavily than evidence that is less salient but equally or more probative. A complainant's distress at interview is vivid. An access log showing the respondent was not in the relevant location at the relevant time is less vivid. The evidence matrix, applied consistently, requires every category of evidence to be assessed against every element of every allegation regardless of its emotional salience.

Evidence from multiple sources requires attention to provenance. Evidence provided by the complainant is not independent. Evidence provided by the respondent is not independent. Evidence retrieved independently from employer systems, third-party records, or witnesses with no prior relationship to the parties carries greater evidential weight because it is not shaped by the interests of the principals.

One further obligation applies at this stage that workplace investigations commonly overlook. The Model Code of Practice on Managing Psychosocial Hazards requires organisations to collect de-identified details of all reports, including those not formally pursued, to identify systemic issues and trends across the workplace. The evidence-gathering phase of an individual investigation is also, from the organisation's WHS perspective, a data-gathering exercise that contributes to the broader picture of what conditions in this workplace are producing. A finding that the individual allegation was unsubstantiated does not discharge the organisation's obligation to understand whether the conditions that gave rise to the complaint represent a systemic hazard. The evidence gathered in the investigation should be assessed for its systemic implications, not only its bearing on the specific allegations.

The Duty to Seek, Not Just Receive

The investigator's obligation is to seek the evidence that is available, not merely to receive what is offered.

This is the distinction the Fair Work Commission drew in *Smout v BHP*, where the failure was not that the investigator ignored evidence presented to him. It was that he did not seek evidence both complainants had indicated existed. A witness had been described. An identification process using attendance records and security photographs was available. The investigator did not pursue it. The Commission found this to be a failure of investigative rigour that beggars belief in a person conducting an independent investigation.

The duty to seek is grounded in both the evidentiary standard and the WHS framework. Under the Burchell Test, a genuine belief in misconduct based on reasonable grounds requires a reasonable investigation. An investigation that did not seek available evidence has not met the reasonable investigation requirement regardless of what it found from the evidence it did seek. Under the WHS Act, evidence gathering is the mechanism through which the organisation discharges its primary duty to understand and control the psychosocial hazard. An investigation that did not seek available evidence has also not discharged that duty.

Where a witness is mentioned by any party, the investigator must make a considered judgment about whether to interview them and record the reason for their decision either way. Where a category of documentary evidence is relevant, it must be sought unless there is a recorded reason why seeking it is disproportionate to its probative value. Where a party indicates that a record exists, the investigator must either retrieve it independently or explain why the party's own copy is being relied upon instead. The test is whether a fair-minded person, knowing what the investigator knew, would have expected the investigation to seek that evidence.

PRACTITIONER NOTE

The evidence-gathering failure most likely to be invisible until it is tested is the record that was not sought.

The investigation that produces a finding based on the evidence it gathered may have gathered only the evidence it expected to find. The email exchange that was retrieved. The witnesses who came forward. The documents the parties provided. The evidence that was not anticipated, not requested, and not found is absent from the matrix not because it does not exist but because nobody asked the question that would have revealed it.

The discipline of asking both the hypothesis question and its inverse at each stage prevents this. If the allegation is true, what records would that have generated? If it is not true, what records would demonstrate that? Both questions should be asked before each evidence category is considered closed. The second question is the one most likely to be skipped when the investigation is running under pressure and the first has already produced a coherent evidence base. It is also the question whose answer most directly determines whether the finding survives challenge.

The second failure is the screenshot accepted as the primary record. The investigation that has accepted screenshots from the complainant, summarised them in the report, and relied on them as evidence without independently retrieving the underlying records has built its finding on evidence whose reliability cannot be assessed. If the underlying records contradict the screenshots, the investigation has no record of having checked. If they confirm them, the investigation has missed the opportunity to strengthen its finding with independently verified evidence. The retrieval takes the same time as accepting screenshots. It produces a fundamentally more defensible record.

The third failure is the environmental assessment not conducted. The physical context of an allegation is evidence that cannot be retrospectively recreated once the investigation closes. The location changes. The equipment is moved. The access records are archived. The assessment of what was possible in that location at that time must be made while the evidence is available.

A NOTE ON COGNITIVE STYLE

Evidence gathering is the phase where the pattern-recognition capacity of a non-linear thinker is most directly useful and most directly dangerous.

The asset is the capacity to see connections across disparate evidence sources: the email record that seems unremarkable until placed alongside the access log and the roster. The gap in the documentation that becomes significant when the witness's account is mapped against the timeline. The contemporaneous message that changes the meaning of the interview account. These connections are not always visible to an analysis that assesses each piece of evidence in isolation. A non-linear thinker who holds multiple evidence streams simultaneously can see them.

The danger is the same capacity applied too early. A pattern recognised from partial evidence is a hypothesis, not a finding. The gathering phase must remain genuinely open to the evidence the pattern does not predict. The investigator who has seen the shape of the allegation in the first round of documents may unconsciously frame subsequent evidence requests to confirm rather than test that shape. The evidence matrix, populated consistently and reviewed before each subsequent evidence request, is the structural check: if the matrix does not contain the evidence that would support the alternative explanation, the inquiry is not complete regardless of how coherent the primary pattern appears.

The investigation log records the decisions made during gathering, including the decision not to pursue particular evidence and the reason why, so that the pattern followed and the pattern not followed are both visible when the finding is assessed.

What Comes Next

The evidence base is being built. Documentary records have been preserved and retrieved. The environmental assessment has been completed. Witness interviews are about to begin.

Chapter Six addresses the interview itself: the methodology for conducting investigative interviews that produce reliable evidence, the cognitive interview framework adapted to the workplace context, and the specific techniques that distinguish an interview that gathers evidence from an interview that confirms an existing view. Interviewing is the phase where most workplace investigations fail, and where the difference between the practitioner who has been trained in investigative methodology and the practitioner who has not is most apparent in the evidence base produced.

Chapter Six

Conducting Interviews

Investigations fail at the interview.

Not because the investigator asks the wrong questions. Because they ask questions at all, in the conventional sense: specific, directed, confirmatory questions that tell the witness what the investigator already thinks happened and invite them to agree or disagree. This is not interviewing. It is the performance of interviewing, and its product is not testimony. It is the witness's response to the investigator's hypothesis, shaped by the authority of the person asking and the conditions of the room in which they are sitting.

The investigative interview, conducted properly, is a cognitive retrieval exercise. The witness has information stored in memory. The investigator's task is to create the conditions under which that information can be retrieved without the retrieval process contaminating what is retrieved. Every technique that feels natural to a practitioner under pressure, leading questions, challenge, confrontation, the rapid-fire sequence of closed questions designed to confirm a timeline, is the technique that degrades the reliability of what the interview produces.

This is not a gentle observation about treating people kindly. Unfair interviews produce unreliable evidence, and the Fair Work Commission applied exactly this principle in *Roy Smout v BHP Coal Pty Ltd* [2024] FWC 2062 when it found that the investigator's use of leading questions, rather than open probing questions, was a failure of investigative rigour that undermined the reliability of the findings the investigation produced.

The natural counterargument is that cognitive interviewing is too time-consuming for routine matters. The answer is that a free narrative phase takes fifteen minutes and produces richer evidence than a forty-question directed interview that takes the same time and produces a record of the investigator's propositions rather than the witness's account. The investment is not in the time. It is in the method.

The Cognitive Interview: Why It Works

The cognitive interview methodology, developed by Fisher and Geiselman (1992), is the evidence-based framework for investigative interviews that produce reliable testimony. It was developed from research into the conditions that support accurate memory retrieval and the conditions that undermine it. Its foundational principles apply directly to workplace investigations, but the full methodology requires adaptation from its criminal justice origins: it is cumbersome in its complete form, and the workplace context introduces procedural obligations and power dynamics that criminal witness interviews do not share. This chapter covers the adapted application.

The methodology rests on four cognitive principles.

Memory is associative. Information stored in memory is linked to the context in which it was encoded: the physical environment, the emotional state, the other people present, the sensory conditions of the moment. Retrieval is most accurate when the conditions of encoding can be approximated at retrieval. This is why mental reinstatement of context produces richer and more accurate recall than asking a witness to describe what they remember without any contextual prompt.

Memory is not a single file. The same event encodes multiple traces across different memory systems. A witness who cannot recall a detail when asked directly may access it through a different retrieval pathway. Asking the witness to describe the event from a different temporal starting point, or from the perspective of another person present, activates different pathways and often produces detail that direct questioning missed.

Memory retrieval is effortful. Accurate recall of a complex event requires sustained cognitive effort that the witness can only maintain in conditions that support concentration. Interruptions, rapid question sequences, and the cognitive load of managing anxiety about the investigator's reaction all reduce the mental resources available for retrieval. The interviewer who tolerates silence, who does not interrupt, who waits for the witness to complete their retrieval before asking another question, produces qualitatively different testimony from the one who drives the interview forward.

Psychological safety is not a welfare consideration. It is an evidentiary requirement. A witness who feels threatened, judged, or controlled by the interview process is managing their own psychological state rather than searching their memory. The reduced working memory capacity that anxiety produces is a fundamental impairment of the cognitive function the interview depends on. Subsequent meta-analytic research on Fisher and Geiselman's methodology has reported gains of approximately 34 per cent in correct details retrieved, with accuracy rates broadly comparable to standard interviewing. The difference is not marginal, and it is not a function of the witness becoming more honest. It is the product of a method designed to support retrieval rather than direct it.

The manner of the interview is itself a regulated matter. The Model Code of Practice on Managing Psychosocial Hazards identifies the manner in which an investigation is conducted as a potential psychosocial hazard. The PCBU has a primary duty of care under the Work Health and Safety Act 2011 to ensure the interview process does not cause psychological harm to the parties involved. An interview conducted with aggression, contempt, or deliberate disregard for the interviewee's dignity is not just a poor interview. It is a process that creates liability for the organisation that commissioned it.

The Four Components of the Cognitive Interview

The cognitive interview is structured around four core components, each targeting a different aspect of the retrieval process. In the workplace investigation context they operate as a sequence.

Mental reinstatement of context

Before the witness begins their account, the investigator asks them to mentally recreate the physical and emotional context of the relevant events: where they were, what they were doing, what the environment was like, how they were feeling. This is a retrieval technique that activates the contextual cues associated with the encoded memory. The machine noise question from *Smout v BHP* illustrates the practical value: a complainant operating loud cleaning equipment at the time of an alleged comment was never asked about the noise conditions. Under cross-examination at the hearing, she acknowledged she had not heard the comment. Mental reinstatement of context, conducted during the interview, would have surfaced this before the finding was made.

Report everything

The investigator instructs the witness to report everything they recall, including details that seem insignificant, partial, or uncertain. The witness's natural tendency is to filter their account, reporting only what seems important and omitting what seems peripheral. This filtering removes the detail that is often the most probative evidence the interview produces. The explicit instruction to report everything counteracts this tendency.

Recall in different order

After the witness has provided their initial account, the investigator asks them to recall the events in a different temporal sequence. This disrupts the tendency to reproduce a rehearsed narrative rather than a retrieved memory. A witness whose account is a rehearsed story will find reverse recall difficult. A witness retrieving genuine memory will find different details accessible from different starting points. The finding you reach with leading questions is a finding the Fair Work Commission will reverse. The finding you reach through a witness's genuinely retrieved, reverse-recalled account is a finding that stands.

Change perspective

The investigator asks the witness to consider the events from the perspective of another person who was present. This accesses information encoded from the witness's visual perspective that they have not reported because they do not recognise its significance from their own viewpoint. In the workplace context it must be used with care where the other person is the subject of a complaint, but applied to peripheral witnesses it produces detail that directed questioning never reaches.

After the free narrative and cognitive components are complete, targeted questions address gaps and inconsistencies. Closed questions have a legitimate role in this final stage: they confirm specific details after open recall is exhausted and create the opportunity to test the account against documentary evidence already in the investigator's possession. The distinction between the free narrative phase and the analytic questioning phase is the structure that gives both their value. The investigator who moves to closed questions before the free narrative is complete has collapsed the structure and lost the evidence the structure was designed to produce.

Interviewing the Complainant

The complainant interview holds two purposes simultaneously: to obtain the most complete and accurate account available, and to conduct the interview in a way that does not compound the harm of the conduct reported. These are not competing purposes. An interview conducted with genuine respect for the complainant's dignity, with control transferred to them, with open questions that invite narrative, produces better evidence because it creates the conditions under which accurate retrieval is possible.

The free narrative phase is the foundation of the complainant interview. The complainant who is invited to tell the investigator everything they can recall, without interruption and without direction, provides an account that is their own. The investigator's first task is to hear that account completely before asking any question. The discipline of not interrupting, not redirecting, not inserting the investigator's framework into the account as it unfolds, is the hardest discipline in investigative interviewing and the most consequential.

The natural behaviour of a witness in an interview with an institutional authority is to stop retrieving their own memory and start responding to what the investigator's questions suggest. This is not deliberate compliance or dishonesty. It is the predictable response to the power differential inherent in the interview. An authority figure who asks specific, directed questions signals what kind of answer is expected, and the witness who feels that signal will produce the expected answer, consciously or not, because responding to authority in an ambiguous situation is how most people manage the cognitive and social demands of the encounter. The free narrative phase removes this signal by removing the questions.

Baselining begins during the rapport-building stage that precedes the substantive account. The investigator who engages the complainant in a brief, genuine, non-investigative conversation before moving to the substantive account has an opportunity to observe how the complainant retrieves and communicates information in conditions of low stakes. That baseline observation provides a reference point for the credibility assessment in Chapter Seven: what does this person look and sound like when they are retrieving a memory they have no reason to misrepresent?

Where the complainant describes conduct that distresses them, the investigator acknowledges the distress, offers a break, and returns when they are ready. A complainant pushed through a distressing account without acknowledgement has less cognitive capacity for the account that follows. The acknowledgement is not a credibility assessment. It is a practical requirement for the evidence that comes after it.

Interviewing Witnesses

The witness interview is the primary site of evidentiary contamination.

A witness who has discussed the events with the complainant, the respondent, or other colleagues before being interviewed has been exposed to post-event information that may have altered their recollection. This may be deliberate or may be the product of ordinary social interaction in a workplace where everyone knows something is happening. People in ambiguous situations look to others to determine what is correct. A witness who has heard the complainant's account does not need to decide consciously to align with it. The alignment occurs through the natural process of constructing a coherent understanding from multiple inputs, and the most recently heard account carries weight in that construction. The investigator who assumes accounts were aligned through collusion may be wrong. The investigator who assumes they were unaffected by contact between the parties is more likely to be wrong.

An investigator who leads a witness is not searching for the truth. They are checking their own work.

A witness asked did you see the respondent speak to the complainant in an aggressive way has been offered a characterisation before they have provided an account. The witness who answers yes has confirmed the characterisation, not retrieved their memory of the event. The open question, what did you observe in the interaction between X and Y, produces an account. The leading question produces a response to a proposition. These are not equivalent forms of evidence.

The specific complication of the witness who has made a prior written statement deserves attention. A witness who has already given a written account, whether a complaint record or a contemporaneous note, has made a commitment that creates psychological pressure to be consistent in the interview. Even where the prior account is incomplete or inaccurate, the witness will feel a pull toward consistency that may prevent them from providing a fuller or more accurate account in the interview. The free narrative phase, conducted without reference to the prior statement, gives the witness the opportunity to retrieve their memory independently. Inconsistencies between the free narrative and the prior statement are then material for the analytic questioning phase, not a reason to confront the witness before the narrative is complete.

Interviewing the Respondent

The respondent interview is the most procedurally complex interview in a workplace investigation.

The procedural requirements are non-negotiable. The respondent must have received the particularised allegations before the interview. They must have had adequate time to consider those allegations and to seek advice. They must have been offered the opportunity to have a support person present, and if they have taken that opportunity, the support person must be present before the interview begins.

The support person's role requires specific clarification. A support person is present for emotional support and as a sounding board. They do not abrogate the respondent's obligation to provide their own responses. They are not legal representation. They cannot answer questions on behalf of the respondent, take over the interview, or prevent the investigator from pursuing a line of questioning. The investigator who allows the support person to dominate the respondent's interview has not provided the respondent with an interview. They have provided the support person with one, and the respondent's right to respond has not been exercised.

The cognitive interview applies to the respondent interview with adaptation. Mental reinstatement of context should be offered: the respondent invited to mentally recreate the events the allegations describe is being invited to retrieve their own memory, not respond to the investigator's characterisation. A respondent whose recollection is retrieved through open cognitive interviewing provides a more complete and more testable account than one whose interview consists of responding to allegations point by point.

The respondent who denies the alleged conduct entirely should be asked to describe what did occur in the relevant context, in enough detail that the account can be assessed against the other evidence available. A respondent who says that conversation never happened should be asked to describe what conversations did take place, when, where, and what was said. The respondent's account of what happened is evidence, even where it contradicts the complainant's account. The assessment of relative reliability on the balance of probabilities is the subject of Chapter Seven, not of the interview itself.

The respondent who refuses to participate has declined the procedural fairness opportunity they were offered. This must be documented, and the investigation must proceed on the evidence available. The refusal is noted. It does not constitute a finding of misconduct or an admission.

Where a respondent discloses counter-allegations in the course of the interview, the investigator notes the disclosure, informs the respondent it will be assessed against the Terms of Reference, and makes a considered decision after the interview about whether the scope should expand. The interview is not redirected mid-session.

Recording the Interview

The interview record is evidence. It requires the same discipline applied to documentary evidence.

A verbatim record, or a record that clearly distinguishes between the witness's language and the investigator's summary, is the standard. The paraphrase is the investigator's interpretation of what was said. That interpretation may reflect the investigator's existing view of the case in ways invisible in the record. When the record is later assessed, inconsistencies between what the witness said and what the investigator recorded as a summary will not be visible. The verbatim record makes the account assessable. The summary makes only the investigator's interpretation of it assessable, which is a different and weaker form of evidence.

Baselining, which begins in the rapport stage, continues through the record phase: the investigator's notes should capture not only what the witness said but the conditions under which they said it, any indications of distress, retrieval difficulty, or uncertainty, and any point at which the witness appeared to be recalling rather than reconstructing. These observations are not credibility findings. They are contextual information that the credibility assessment in Chapter Seven will draw on.

At the conclusion of the interview, the witness should be given the opportunity to review the record and sign off on it. This is not an opportunity to revise their account. It is the confirmation that the record accurately captures what they said. A witness who has reviewed and confirmed the accuracy of their record provides stronger evidence than one whose record was created without review. Where a correction is made, the original record and the correction should both be preserved: the fact of the correction, what was changed and why, is itself potentially relevant.

Procedural Fairness in the Interview Process

Every interview in a workplace investigation is a procedural fairness event as well as an evidentiary one.

For the complainant, procedural fairness in the interview means being heard fully and without interruption, being treated with dignity throughout, and not being asked to justify their decision to make a complaint. A complainant who leaves the interview feeling their account was not taken seriously has received a signal about the investigation's integrity that will affect their confidence in the outcome.

For the respondent, procedural fairness means receiving the allegations before the interview, having adequate preparation time, having a support person if they want one, having an investigator conducting a genuine inquiry rather than seeking confirmation, and having their account recorded accurately. These are the requirements of natural justice applied to the interview stage.

For all parties, informational fairness during the interview stage means being told what will happen with their account, what the process involves from this point, and what the expected timeframe is. Keeping people informed about matters that affect them is a pillar of organisational justice. Leaving parties in silence about what happens after the interview creates anxiety that compounds the stress of the process itself.

Intersectionality and Adaptation

The standard cognitive interview is designed for a cognitively typical interviewee in a psychologically safe environment. Most interviews in workplace investigations involve neither.

Where a party or witness is neurodivergent, the components of the cognitive interview most dependent on working memory require adaptation. Research on interviewing neurodivergent witnesses identifies mental reinstatement of context, change order, and change perspective as the components perceived as most difficult, specifically because they depend on the working memory capacity that non-linear profiles most affect. The components perceived as most effective, establish rapport, open non-leading questions, and compatible questions timed to the interviewee's cognitive pace, are the foundation of the adapted approach.

For a neurodivergent interviewee: extend the time allocated, reduce or eliminate the most cognitively demanding components, allow longer pauses without interpreting them as reluctance or evasion, use simpler and more direct language, and offer the option of a written account before or after the interview. Memory retrieval difficulty in a neurodivergent interviewee is not evasion. It is the product of the interaction between cognitive profile and interview conditions. An investigator who cannot distinguish between the two has produced an unreliable credibility assessment before the interview has concluded.

Where a party or witness belongs to a marginalised group, the investigator must be aware of the specific vulnerabilities that intersecting identities can create. A person from a cultural and linguistic minority background may face the power imbalance inherent in the interview and the additional barrier of cultural distance between their communication norms and the investigator's expectations. An LGBTQIA witness may be experiencing minority stress that affects their capacity to engage with an institutional process. The investigator who assumes the standard approach works equally for everyone applies a standard that advantages some and disadvantages others.

The practical requirement is reflexivity. Before each interview, the investigator considers what factors specific to this person in this context might affect the quality of their account, and makes deliberate decisions about how to address those factors. The investigator who has done this has met the standard. The investigator who has assumed the standard approach is universally applicable has not.

Sustaining the Standard Across an Interview Programme

The principle that psychological state is an evidentiary variable applies symmetrically. A witness whose working memory is compromised by anxiety produces less reliable testimony. An interviewer whose working memory is compromised by accumulated cognitive load produces less effective interviews. The mechanism is the same. The implications for the investigation are different but no less material.

An investigation programme of any complexity will require multiple interviews across several weeks. Each interview, properly conducted, requires the interviewer to sustain attentive listening through the free narrative phase, to suspend the analytic frame they bring to the file, to hold the alternative hypothesis open while the account develops, and to baseline the witness's retrieval style in the rapport stage. This is cognitively demanding work. The fourth interview of the week, conducted after two days of document review and the cumulative weight of distressing accounts received earlier, is being conducted under conditions that reduce the interviewer's capacity to apply the method the chapter has described. The interviewer is rarely aware that this is happening. The quality of the interview reflects it regardless.

The practical implications are not pastoral. They are operational. Interview density should be managed: more than two substantive interviews in a single day is the upper limit of what most practitioners can sustain at the required standard. Recovery time between interviews is part of the interviewing methodology, not a separate welfare matter. The investigator who is conducting a complainant interview about distressing conduct should not be conducting another substantive interview within the same day, and the investigator who is approaching the end of an extended interview programme should be alert to the signs that their own capacity has degraded: reading rather than listening, defaulting to the directed questioning the chapter cautions against, finding the silence in the free narrative phase intolerable rather than productive.

Where the volume of interviews exceeds what a single practitioner can sustain, the appropriate response is to assign a second investigator rather than compress the schedule. The handbook's structural elements, the plan, the evidence matrix, the investigation log, the verbatim interview records, support continuity between investigators where one is required to step out of the programme. The standard is what protects the investigation. The structural support is what protects the standard, including from the cumulative cognitive load of the work itself.

PRACTITIONER NOTE

The interview failure most likely to be invisible in the record is the one caused by the questions rather than the answers.

A witness interview consisting of forty closed questions and forty confirmatory responses looks, on paper, like a thorough interview. The investigator covered every element of every allegation. The witness confirmed or denied each one. The record is complete. What the record does not show is that the witness never had the opportunity to provide an account, only the opportunity to respond to the investigator's propositions. The information the witness actually holds was never accessed because the questions never reached it.

The single most powerful change a practitioner can make is to begin with a free narrative phase: a block of uninterrupted time in which the witness is invited to tell the investigator everything they can recall about the relevant events, without any questions other than what else and tell me more about that. The free narrative produces less structured but far richer evidence than a directed interview. It accesses what the witness knows rather than what the investigator expected them to know.

The second failure is the interview conducted by video or telephone without awareness of what that format removes. Telephone interviews for complainants were found totally inappropriate by Commissioner Riordan in Smout v BHP because body language is an essential component of every interview. The investigator conducting a telephone interview has no access to the non-verbal communication that signals distress, uncertainty, or evasion, and cannot observe whether another person is present in the room or whether the witness is reading from a prepared account. Where the nature and seriousness of the allegations warrant it, face-to-face interviews produce qualitatively different evidence and should be the default.

The third failure is the record that summarises rather than records. The summary that says the witness confirmed that the respondent made comments of a sexual nature has recorded the investigator's characterisation of the witness's account, not the account itself. When the finding based on that record is challenged, the question of what the witness actually said, and whether the characterisation is accurate, cannot be answered from the record. The record should contain what the witness said. The characterisation belongs in the assessment.

A NOTE ON COGNITIVE STYLE

The investigative interview is the phase where the cognitive profile of a non-linear thinker produces its most direct and most complex interaction with the investigation's requirements.

The asset is the capacity to hold multiple evidence streams simultaneously and to notice when the witness's account does not fit the pattern established by other evidence. The non-linear interviewer who has reviewed the documentary evidence before the interview enters the session with a complete picture that allows them to hear what is absent from the witness's account as clearly as what is present. The inconsistency between the account and the access log. The detail the witness provides that was not in the complaint record and that suggests direct knowledge of the event. These are the connections that document-first preparation and cognitive presence make visible.

The danger is the same capacity deployed as a confirmation engine. The non-linear thinker whose picture is complete before the interview begins is at risk of conducting an interview that confirms the picture rather than tests it. The questions that feel most natural are the ones that address the gaps in the existing narrative. The cognitive interview's free narrative phase is the structural defence against this: it prevents the investigator from driving the account before the witness has had the opportunity to produce one.

The bias check from Chapter Three applies with force here. Before each interview: what would I hear from this witness if my current view of the case is wrong? What account would they give that I am not expecting? What would I do with that account? These are not comfortable questions when the evidence already has a clear shape. They are the questions that determine whether the interview is an inquiry or a confirmation exercise.

What Comes Next

The interview programme is complete. The complainant has been heard. The witnesses have given their accounts. The respondent has had a genuine opportunity to respond to the particularised allegations. The records are verbatim and reviewed. The evidence matrix is populated with what each interview produced.

Chapter Seven addresses the assessment of that evidence: the credibility framework, the alternative hypothesis test applied to the assembled evidence base, and the disciplined reasoning that distinguishes a defensible finding from a confirmed assumption. Most investigations fail at the finding. The assessment is where the standard the handbook has established is either applied or quietly set aside.

Chapter Seven

Assessing Evidence

Most investigations fail at the finding.

Not through bad evidence. Through flawed reasoning about good evidence. The gathering phase is complete. The interviews are done. The documents have been reviewed. One account is more detailed, more consistent, and more plausible than the other. The finding writes itself. What has not happened, and what the investigative standard requires, is the articulation of the strongest alternative explanation for the evidence, and the assessment of whether the evidence eliminates that alternative as the more probable account. The feeling of obvious is not a finding. It is the point at which the work begins.

The counterargument is that this level of rigour is unnecessary for minor internal matters. The counterargument is wrong. There are no minor internal matters when the finding is challenged. The standard a workplace investigation is held to does not scale with the seniority of the parties, the size of the organisation, or the confidence of the investigator. It scales with the consequence to the people inside it, and those consequences are never minor.

The Standard of Proof

The standard of proof in workplace investigations is the civil standard: the balance of probabilities. A fact is proved on the balance of probabilities if its existence is more probable than not. This is the standard that governs civil litigation, employment disputes, and the great majority of decisions made in Australian workplaces.

What makes it demanding in the investigation context is not the threshold but the discipline required to apply it honestly. The balance of probabilities requires that the investigator assess what the evidence shows, not what they believe happened. A belief that the respondent engaged in the alleged conduct, formed before the evidence has been assessed, is not a finding at the standard. It is a conclusion reached before any process has been applied, and it is vulnerable to challenge.

The Burchell Test translates the civil standard into the investigation's practical requirement: the employer must demonstrate a genuine belief in the misconduct, based on reasonable grounds, established through a reasonable investigation. A genuine belief based on insufficient grounds is not enough. Reasonable grounds established without a reasonable investigation are not enough. The three elements together define what a finding at the civil standard looks like when it is examined by the Fair Work Commission under s.387 of the Fair Work Act 2009.

One common failure in applying the standard is the treatment of unsubstantiated as the equivalent to false. A finding that an allegation is unsubstantiated means the evidence does not support it on the balance of probabilities. It does not mean the conduct did not occur. It does not mean the complainant fabricated the account. The distinction matters to the complainant who receives it, to the respondent whose record it concerns, and to the organisation's post-investigation obligations, which do not disappear because the disciplinary finding was unsubstantiated. The language of findings must be precise: what was found, on what standard, and what that finding does and does not establish.

The Alternative Hypothesis Test

The alternative hypothesis test is the discipline that distinguishes a finding from a conclusion.

Before finalising any finding, the investigator must perform a specific intellectual exercise: articulate the strongest explanation for the available evidence other than the finding being reached, and assess whether the evidence, weighed as a whole, eliminates that alternative as the more probable account on the balance of probabilities. This is not the elimination of all theoretical possibility. It is the assessment of whether the alternative explanation is less probable than the finding, given the evidence available.

The test operates in both directions. For a finding that the alleged conduct occurred, the investigator must identify and assess the strongest alternative explanation for the evidence that supports that conclusion. For a finding that the conduct cannot be established, the investigator must identify and assess the evidence that would support a finding in the other direction, and explain why that evidence does not, on the balance of probabilities, support the allegation.

The specific failure the test is designed to prevent is the finding driven by coherence rather than evidence. The mind constructs narratives from available information and treats the coherence of the narrative as evidence of its truth. A coherent account feels like a correct account. A comprehensive evidence base feels like a complete one. What the mind is blind to is what it has not seen: the evidence excluded by the narrative, the alternative explanation the story does not accommodate. The alternative hypothesis test is the deliberate act of looking for what the primary narrative excludes, before the finding is written, while there is still time to test it.

The *Courtney Sewell v dnata Airport Services Pty Limited* [2025] FWC 2823 decision provides the clearest available illustration of what the failure to apply this test produces. The investigator treated evidence as misaligned where the complainant's and respondent's accounts differed and recorded findings as unable to be substantiated as a result. The Commission found this a serious flaw: the investigator had treated conflicting accounts as the endpoint of the assessment rather than as evidence to be weighed. The alternative hypothesis test, applied to the evidence as a whole, including the complainant's contemporaneous emotional state and immediate disclosure to colleagues, would have required the investigator to assess whether misalignment was itself the most probable explanation for the evidence, or whether one account was more probably correct than the other on the available material.

The Credibility Assessment

In most workplace investigations the primary evidence is testimonial and the accounts conflict. The credibility assessment is the process by which the investigator determines what weight to give each account.

Credibility assessment is an assessment of the reliability of a witness's account: how accurately does this account reflect what the witness actually observed and experienced? It is not an assessment of the witness's character, their employment history, or whether the investigator finds them sympathetic. These distinctions are not merely ethical. They are evidentiary: an assessment of character in place of an assessment of reliability produces a finding based on the wrong question.

The legitimate indicators of credibility are specific and should be applied consistently.

Internal consistency

The degree to which the witness's account is consistent across the interview: whether the account told at the beginning is consistent with the account provided at the end, whether the witness's description of their emotional response is consistent with their description of their actions. Inconsistency within a single account is a credibility indicator. It is not, by itself, a finding of dishonesty: a witness retrieving a complex memory under pressure may sequence events differently at different points without that inconsistency indicating fabrication.

External consistency

The degree to which the witness's account is consistent with independent evidence: documents, access records, contemporaneous messages, the accounts of other witnesses who had no opportunity to align. External consistency is the most probative credibility indicator available because it tests the account against evidence created without knowledge of how it would be used. A specific principle applies here: evidence that has not been challenged or disputed and that is not inherently incredible ought to be accepted. Where one party's account has been corroborated by independent evidence and the other party has not challenged that corroboration, the weight of the unchallenged evidence is substantial and should be recorded as such in the assessment.

Opportunity to observe

The assessment of whether the witness could actually have observed what they claim to have observed, given the physical circumstances of the event. The machine noise question from *Smout v BHP* is the clearest illustration: a witness operating loud equipment may not have been able to hear the comment she claimed to have heard. Assessing the plausibility of the account in the context of the physical environment is the application of the investigative standard to the question of what was possible.

Prior consistent statements

Disclosures made before the investigation began or before the witness had reason to align their account with a preferred outcome. A complainant who disclosed the conduct to a colleague immediately after it occurred has produced a prior consistent statement independent of anything they say in the interview. The weight of that disclosure in the credibility assessment is substantial because it was created before the investigation and before any interest in the outcome had been engaged.

Motive to misrepresent

The assessment of whether the witness has a reason to give an account that is other than accurate. The existence of a motive does not establish that the witness has misrepresented. Many people with strong reasons to be less than accurate give accurate accounts. The indicator is one factor in the overall assessment, not a determinative one.

The credibility indicators that are not legitimate are as important as those that are, because they are the ones most commonly applied.

Demeanour is not credibility

An investigator who relies on demeanour is not assessing credibility. They are recording their own emotional reaction and calling it a finding. A witness who is visibly distressed may be distressed because they experienced what they described, or because they are anxious about a formal process, or because they are a person who experiences distress easily. A witness who is calm may be calm because their account is considered and accurate, or because they are not being truthful about something that does not distress them. The emotional presentation of the witness during the interview is not evidence of the accuracy of their account.

Seniority or status is not credibility

The account of a senior manager does not carry more weight than the account of a junior employee. The account of an employee with no disciplinary history does not carry more weight than the account of one who has had performance issues. These are character assessments, and character assessments produce findings that reflect institutional hierarchies rather than evidentiary reasoning.

Neurodivergent behaviour is not credibility

A neurodivergent witness or party may present with working memory gaps, chronological inconsistency across the interview, difficulty with change-order recall, or a fragmented communication style. None of these features are indicators of unreliability. They are the product of the interaction between cognitive profile and the formal interview environment. An investigator who treats non-linear associated behaviours as credibility deficits has assessed the person's neurodivergence rather than the reliability of their account, and the finding that follows will reflect that error rather than the evidence.

Subjective impression is not credibility

The feeling that a witness is telling the truth, formed during the interview and not traceable to any specific feature of their account or any specific inconsistency with independent evidence, is the availability heuristic operating as a credibility assessment. The vivid, engaging, emotionally resonant account feels true. The flat, clinical account feels rehearsed. Neither feeling is evidence.

The Cognitive Bias Cluster

Three cognitive biases are responsible for most evidentiary assessment failures in workplace investigations. Each is well-established in cognitive psychology and well-documented in formal investigative settings. They operate below the level of deliberate reasoning and are most active when the investigator is most confident they are reasoning carefully.

Confirmation bias, first formally characterised in psychological research by Wason (1960) and developed across subsequent decades by Tversky, Kahneman, and Nickerson, is the tendency to seek, weight, and retain evidence that supports a conclusion already formed, and to discount or misinterpret evidence that challenges it. In the investigation context it typically presents not as a deliberate distortion of evidence but as a sequence of small framing decisions: the question phrased in a way that assumes the answer, the documentary evidence collected from sources most likely to support the primary account, the inconsistency in the respondent's account noted while the inconsistency in the complainant's account is explained. Each decision looks reasonable. The pattern it produces does not.

The availability heuristic, identified by Tversky and Kahneman (1973), is the tendency to weight evidence according to how readily it comes to mind rather than how probative it is. A complainant's distress at interview is vivid and easily recalled. An access log showing the respondent was not in the relevant location requires deliberate effort to retrieve and weight appropriately. The evidence matrix, reviewed before the final finding is written, is the structural intervention: it forces every category of evidence to be assessed against every element of every allegation regardless of emotional salience.

Fundamental attribution error, named by Ross (1977) and developed in the social psychology literature since, is the tendency to explain other people's behaviour as a product of their character rather than their circumstances. In the investigation context it most often distorts the assessment of the respondent's conduct: the respondent who made a comment is assessed as a person who makes those kinds of comments, rather than as a person who made a comment in a specific context that may or may not reflect a pattern. The assessment should address the conduct alleged and the evidence that supports or contradicts its occurrence. It should not extend to characterisations of the respondent as a person.

A fourth bias warrants specific attention alongside these three. The investigator's emotional response to the source of evidence, distinct from its content, affects how they weight it. Evidence provided by a person the investigator respects, trusts, or finds credible as a professional will be intuitively treated as more reliable than equivalent evidence from a person the investigator distrusts. This is not a deliberate error. It is the predictable product of an assessment process that is not fully separated from the investigator's prior impressions of the parties, and it is a specific reason why the evidence matrix, which requires the investigator to record what the evidence shows rather than how they received it, is the primary structural defence against this form of bias.

Conflicting Accounts and the Balance of Probabilities

The investigation where the complainant's account and the respondent's account directly contradict each other, with no independent witness and limited documentary evidence, is the investigation that most consistently produces assessment failures. The investigator, faced with two internally consistent accounts that cannot both be correct, records an unsubstantiated finding because the evidence does not resolve the conflict.

This conclusion is not a finding. It is an abdication.

Investigators reach for unsubstantiated to avoid making hard calls. The civil standard does not require the conflict to be resolved by independent evidence. It requires the investigator to assess, on the available evidence as a whole, which account is more probable. That assessment draws on the full range of legitimate credibility indicators: which account is internally consistent, which is externally consistent with the available documentary evidence, which is supported by prior consistent statements, which account of the physical circumstances is plausible, and whether either party has a motive to misrepresent that is explained or not explained by their account.

A specific technique assists this assessment without triggering the commitment-and-consistency problem that can make direct confrontation counterproductive. Where a witness's account contains an internal inconsistency, the investigator can offer a natural opportunity to clarify: I want to make sure I have understood you correctly, earlier you said X and later you said Y, can you help me understand that. This gives the witness the opportunity to clarify or correct without being required to formally retract a prior statement. The clarification that follows is more reliable than a correction extracted through direct confrontation, and the witness's response to the opportunity provides its own information about the reliability of the account.

The *Roy Smout v BHP Coal Pty Ltd* [2024] FWC 2062 decision illustrates how the assessment operates in practice. Commissioner Riordan found that two complainants whose accounts were internally consistent, externally consistent with contemporaneous notes, and whose account of specific conduct was internally plausible, provided more reliable evidence than a respondent whose denial was inconsistent in ways the investigation did not adequately probe. The Commission did not require a third-party witness to resolve the conflict. It assessed the relative reliability of the available accounts against the available evidence and reached a finding on the balance of probabilities.

Systemic Implications of the Evidence

A finding that an individual allegation is not substantiated does not resolve the question of whether the workplace conditions that gave rise to the complaint represent an ongoing risk.

The Model Code of Practice on Managing Psychosocial Hazards is explicit: even where a specific breach of conduct is not proven, an underlying work health and safety risk may exist and must be controlled. The investigation that closes the file on a finding of not substantiated, without assessing whether the conditions that produced the complaint reflect a systemic hazard, has not discharged the organisation's obligations.

The evidentiary assessment phase is the appropriate point at which to note any systemic implications: patterns of conduct not individually actionable but that together suggest a workplace culture creating risk, power dynamics that may persist regardless of the individual finding, or organisational conditions that contributed to the complaint or prevented it from being addressed earlier. These observations are not findings about individual conduct. They are the investigation's contribution to the organisation's understanding of what the evidence revealed beyond the specific allegation.

PRACTITIONER NOTE

The evidentiary assessment failure most likely to produce a challenge is the one that feels like the easiest path through the evidence.

The finding that writes itself is the finding that requires the most deliberate application of the alternative hypothesis test. The easier the finding feels, the more likely it is that the conclusion was reached before the reasoning process was completed. The test is not whether the finding is correct. It is whether the finding was reached through a process that assessed the alternative and found it less probable, rather than through a process that never considered the alternative because the primary account was compelling.

The specific experience from investigative practice is that this failure is most acute in cases involving a power imbalance between the parties. The junior employee's account of conduct by a senior employee is assessed through the lens of what the senior employee would and would not do, informed by everything the investigator knows about their reputation and standing. The assessment feels like careful contextual reasoning. It is often confirmation bias operating through a professional frame.

The second failure is investigators reach for not substantiated to avoid making hard calls. The investigation where one account is more probably correct and the investigator records not substantiated because the conflict is unresolved has not applied the civil standard. It has avoided applying it. The finding must reflect the actual assessment. Where the evidence was assessed and found insufficient, the finding says so and explains why. Where the assessment was avoided because the conflict felt irresolvable, the finding is not a finding. It is a record of the investigation having stopped where the work was hardest.

One further observation belongs here, not as a separate point but as the context within which the discipline this chapter describes is sustained.

Making a finding at the balance of probabilities under genuine evidentiary uncertainty is among the heaviest parts of an investigation. The practitioner sits with the awareness that the finding will affect the working life of one or both parties, that the evidence does not fully resolve what occurred, and that the decision must nonetheless be made. The weight is real. The alternative hypothesis test is not only an intellectual discipline. It is the structural support that lets the practitioner make the call by reference to a method rather than by reference to their personal certainty, which would not be sufficient grounds in any case. The discipline does not remove the weight. It distributes it from the practitioner's judgment to the method the practitioner is applying, which is what makes the work sustainable across an investigation programme.

A NOTE ON COGNITIVE STYLE

Evidentiary assessment is the phase where the pattern-recognition capacity of a non-linear thinker is simultaneously most useful and most exposed to the risk of premature closure.

The asset is the capacity to see the evidential picture as a whole: to hold all the evidence streams simultaneously and assess their cumulative weight rather than evaluating each piece in isolation. A non-linear thinker who has absorbed the full evidence base may reach a conclusion that a linear analysis would take longer to arrive at, and that conclusion may be correct. The problem is that the feeling of seeing the whole picture is indistinguishable from the feeling of having formed a premature one.

The alternative hypothesis test is the structural defence. Before writing the finding, the investigator constructs the strongest counter-narrative from the same evidence: what would the evidence look like if the primary account is wrong? What alternative explanation is available? Is that alternative less probable, on the balance of probabilities, than the finding being reached? The counter-narrative that cannot be constructed is evidence that the finding has not been tested. The counter-narrative that can be constructed but that the evidence does not support is the demonstration that the alternative hypothesis test has been applied and the finding is defensible.

The evidence matrix, reviewed in full before the finding is written, prevents the availability heuristic from determining which evidence the finding is based on by making the full evidence base visible at the moment of assessment. The empty cell is part of the assessment. The finding must be defensible in light of what the matrix contains and what it does not.

What Comes Next

The evidence has been assessed. The credibility framework has been applied. The alternative hypothesis test has been completed. The findings have been formulated. The systemic observations have been noted.

Chapter Eight addresses the architecture of the finding itself: the six components that together constitute a defensible finding, the language that distinguishes evidentiary statement from characterisation, and the discipline of writing findings that establish what the evidence shows without reaching beyond it. The assessment has determined what the evidence supports. The finding is how that determination is recorded in a form a decision-maker can rely on and a reviewer can examine.

Chapter Eight

Making Findings

Most investigation reports fail because they are not defensible.

Not because the finding is wrong. Because the report cannot demonstrate it is right. The investigator has gathered coherent evidence. The conclusion that the evidence supports is clear. The finding is written in the language of authority. What the report does not contain, and what the decision-maker who acts on it needs, is the reasoning that produced the conclusion: the evidence addressed against each element of the allegation, the weight assigned and why, the alternative explanation considered and rejected, and the conclusion that follows from the preceding analysis rather than preceding it.

The finding that skips this structure does not save time. It creates the appearance of a defensible outcome without the substance of one. When it is challenged, the investigator discovers that their confidence in the finding is not the same thing as the evidential foundation it required.

There is a specific cognitive mechanism behind this failure, and it has a name. The curse of knowledge, identified by Camerer, Loewenstein, and Weber (1989), describes the difficulty experts have in imagining what others do not yet know. Once an investigator has lived with the evidence through weeks of gathering and assessment, they have forgotten what it is like not to know it. The reasoning steps feel unnecessary because the conclusion is clear. They are not unnecessary. They are the evidence that the investigative standard was applied, and they are what the decision-maker needs to act with confidence and what the Commission will look for when the decision is challenged.

The counterargument is that documenting every element of the reasoning produces bloated reports that serve no one. The counterargument is wrong. A finding that addresses each component in sequence, the allegation, the evidence, the weight, the alternative, the conclusion, is shorter and more navigable than a narrative that circles around to the same conclusion through three paragraphs of impression and characterisation. Structure serves brevity. It does not undermine it.

What a Finding Must Contain

A finding in a workplace investigation is a structured analytical conclusion. It has six components. Each is necessary. None substitutes for another.

1. The allegation as particularised

The finding addresses the allegation as stated in the Terms of Reference, not a broader or narrower version of it. If the allegation was that on a specific date, in a specific location, the respondent said specific words to a specific person, the finding addresses whether that conduct occurred on that date, in that location, in those terms. A finding that addresses something more general than the particularised allegation has answered a question the investigation was not asked. A finding that addresses something narrower has not answered the question it was asked.

2. The evidence relevant to each element

Each element of the allegation, the conduct, the time and place, the parties, the applicable standard, is addressed against the specific evidence that bears on it. The finding records what the evidence shows, not what the investigator concluded from it. The recording of the evidence and the assessment of what it means are separate steps, and the two must be distinguishable in the finding.

3. The weight assigned to the evidence and why

Where evidence conflicts, the finding records which evidence was preferred and the reasons for that preference, applying the legitimate credibility indicators from Chapter Seven. The reasoning must be traceable: not that the complainant appeared more credible, which is a demeanour assessment, but that the complainant's account was consistent with the contemporaneous message record and the respondent's account was not, which is an evidential assessment.

4. The alternative explanation considered and why it was not preferred

The alternative hypothesis test is not an internal quality check. Its output belongs in the finding. The finding must record what the strongest alternative explanation for the evidence was, and why the evidence supports the finding reached rather than the alternative. A finding that does not address the alternative cannot demonstrate the alternative was considered. The decision-maker who relies on it, and the Commission that reviews it, will draw the obvious inference.

5. The conclusion on the balance of probabilities

The conclusion follows from the preceding four components. It does not precede them. A conclusion stated before the evidence has been addressed, the weight assigned, and the alternative considered, is not a finding at the civil standard. It is the investigator's belief expressed in the language of a finding.

6. The policy or standard breach

After determining whether the conduct occurred, the finding addresses whether the proven conduct constitutes a breach of the specific standard cited in the Terms of Reference: the relevant code of conduct, policy, or legislative provision. The finding of fact and the finding of breach are separate analytical steps. A finding that establishes the conduct occurred but does not assess whether it meets the threshold for a breach has not completed the analysis the decision-maker needs to act.

The Three Categories of Finding

Chapter Seven introduced the three categories of finding in the context of assessment. They are returned to here for a different reason: the language of a finding will be acted upon by people who were not present for the investigation, and the precise category recorded determines what the decision-maker, the complainant, and the respondent are entitled to understand the investigation to have produced.

Substantiated

The evidence supports the allegation on the balance of probabilities. The conduct alleged is more probable than not to have occurred, and the evidence establishing that conclusion has been identified, weighed, and tested against the alternative explanation. For a finding of substantiated misconduct to be complete, it must also address the objective test: would a reasonable person, having regard to all the circumstances, consider the conduct unreasonable? The subjective experience of the complainant is relevant to whether the conduct was unwelcome. The objective test determines whether it meets the legal threshold for misconduct.

Not substantiated

The evidence does not support the allegation on the balance of probabilities. The evidence was assessed, the alternative explanation was considered, and the evidence does not establish that the alleged conduct occurred at the applicable standard. This is not a finding that the conduct did not occur. It is not a finding that the complainant was dishonest. It is a finding that the evidence does not meet the standard.

Unable to be determined

The evidence is so sparse, or the reliability of the available accounts so indeterminate given the evidence assessed, that no conclusion can be reached on the balance of probabilities. This is a different finding from not substantiated. A not substantiated finding has been assessed and found insufficient. An unable to be determined finding has not been resolved, and the organisation's post-investigation obligations are not discharged by it.

The Fair Work Commission addressed the consequences of imprecise language directly in *Courtney Sewell v dnata Airport Services Pty Limited* [2025] FWC 2823. The outcome letter described the findings as unable to make a finding for some of the allegations, language so ambiguous the complainant could not determine whether her complaint had been assessed or dismissed. The Commission found this ambiguity contributed to the constructive dismissal outcome. Language in a finding is not a stylistic choice. It is a legal act with consequences for the people it describes and the decision-maker who acts on it.

What a Finding Must Not Contain

A finding must be as precise in what it excludes as in what it includes.

Characterisations of the parties as people

An investigator who characterises a respondent's integrity is not finding a fact. They are providing the respondent with the grounds for an appeal. The finding you write with emotive characterisation today is the Fair Work Commission reversal you will explain to your CEO tomorrow. The termination letter in *Roy Smout v BHP Coal Pty Ltd* [2024] FWC 2062 stated that the respondent's failure to take responsibility for his actions coupled with his lack of integrity raises serious concerns. The Commissioner found the investigation partially flawed. Characterisations that go beyond what the evidence establishes are not findings. They are the investigator's assessment of character, and they are vulnerable to challenge because they exceed what the evidence supports.

Mitigating circumstances

Mitigating factors, workload, personal circumstances, lack of training, are not relevant to whether the conduct occurred. They are relevant to the decision-maker's assessment of the appropriate disciplinary response. The investigator who includes mitigating factors in the finding of fact has conflated the evidentiary question with the disciplinary one. These observations belong in a separate section of the report addressed to the decision-maker, not in the finding itself.

Conclusions about matters outside the Terms of Reference

The finding addresses the allegations in the Terms of Reference. Where the investigation has revealed conduct outside the scope, the mechanism for addressing it is a recommendation to expand the scope or refer to a separate process, not a finding. A finding that addresses conduct outside the Terms of Reference has not given the respondent adequate notice or an adequate opportunity to respond to that conduct, and it will fail the hearing rule on that basis.

The disciplinary recommendation

The finding establishes what the evidence shows. The appropriate disciplinary response is the decision-maker's function. An investigator who includes a disciplinary recommendation has conflated the fact-finding role with the decision-making role. The finding may note the seriousness of the conduct established. It does not recommend the outcome.

Emotive language and demeanour observations

The investigation report records findings of fact, not the investigator's impressions of how the parties presented. A finding that records the complainant appeared visibly distressed and credible throughout the interview has recorded a demeanour observation as if it were evidence. The credibility assessment belongs in the reasoning section, derived from the legitimate credibility indicators, not from the investigator's impression of the witness's emotional state.

Partial Findings

Where an allegation contains multiple elements, the evidence may support a finding on some elements and not others. A partial finding is not a failure of the investigation. It is the investigation applying the standard to the evidence available for each discrete question the allegation asks.

The specific failure to avoid is the partial finding recorded as not substantiated when the correct record is substantiated in part and not substantiated in part, with the elements addressed in each category clearly identified. A finding that records not substantiated where three of five elements were established leaves the decision-maker without the information they need to determine whether a valid reason for disciplinary action exists in relation to the elements that were established.

The unchallenged evidence principle applies here with specific force. Where a respondent has not challenged or disputed specific elements of the evidence, those elements that are not inherently incredible ought to be accepted. The partial finding that records an element as not substantiated when the respondent has not contested the evidence bearing on it has not applied the standard. It has avoided applying it to the uncontested element by treating the contested and uncontested elements as equivalently uncertain.

Roy Smout v BHP Coal Pty Ltd is instructive on the partial finding question. Commissioner Riordan found allegations 1 and 2 substantiated but allegation 3 not substantiated. The investigation had recorded all three as substantiated. The Commission's own assessment produced a different result on one allegation, and that difference affected the overall assessment of the investigation's reliability. A partial finding accurately stated is more defensible than a finding that overstates what the evidence establishes.

Finding in the Absence of Direct Evidence

The absence of direct evidence does not prevent a finding. It requires a more careful application of the alternative hypothesis test and a more precise articulation of the reasoning that produces the conclusion.

The balance of probabilities does not require overwhelming evidence. It requires that one explanation be more probable than the other on the evidence available. The margin between them is often slight, and the law accommodates that: a feather's weight on one side is sufficient to discharge the standard. A finding based on a preference between conflicting accounts, supported by the full range of legitimate credibility indicators, is a finding at the civil standard from testimonial evidence. A finding that records only that the complainant's account is preferred, without the reasoning that supports that preference, is not.

The unchallenged evidence principle applies here: where a witness's account has not been disputed and is not inherently incredible, it carries the weight an unchallenged account commands. The investigator should record, in the finding, whether the respondent has actually disputed each specific element of the evidence, because the weight available to undisputed elements is distinct from the weight available to disputed ones.

The *Sewell* decision is the clearest available statement of this principle. The Commission found that allegations can be substantiated on the balance of probabilities even where no independent witness exists and documentary evidence is limited, if the evidence as a whole supports the finding. The investigator's failure in that case was not the absence of evidence. It was the refusal to apply the standard to the evidence that existed.

When the Investigation Reveals More Than It Was Asked

An investigation conducted rigorously will sometimes reveal conduct beyond the scope of the original complaint. This creates an obligation the investigator must address before the investigation closes.

The first question is whether the additional conduct falls within the existing Terms of Reference. If it does, it should be addressed in the findings.

The second question, where the conduct falls outside the existing scope, is whether the Terms of Reference should be expanded. This is a decision for the person who commissioned the investigation. The investigator's obligation is to bring the additional conduct to their attention, explain what was disclosed, and to recommend whether or not the scope should be expanded. If the commissioning authority decides not to expand the scope, then the investigator must record that decision in the investigation log and proceed within the existing Terms of Reference.

The third question operates parallel to the first two: whether the additional conduct disclosed represents a systemic issue that must be addressed through the organisation's WHS framework regardless of the disciplinary finding. Conduct revealing a pattern, a management failure, or an organisational condition that creates ongoing psychosocial risk is not resolved by the individual investigation's finding. The investigator who notes these systemic implications in the report, as distinct from the individual conduct findings, is discharging an obligation that exists independently of the disciplinary outcome. Where the systemic implications relate to a psychosocial hazard, the organisation has a mandatory duty to consult affected workers on how that hazard will be controlled, under s.35 of the Occupational Health and Safety Act 2004 (Vic) and s.47 of the Work Health and Safety Act 2011 (Cth).

The Finding and the Decision-Maker

The investigator's finding is the input to the decision-maker's process. It is not the decision.

The decision-maker who receives a finding of substantiated serious misconduct must still conduct a separate process: notifying the respondent of the proposed action, giving them a genuine opportunity to respond to that proposed action under s.387(c) of the Fair Work Act 2009, and considering that response before the decision is finalised. The investigation's finding does not authorise the decision-maker to skip this process. It provides the evidentiary foundation for the show cause process that follows.

The finding must be communicated to the parties in a reasonable timeframe. This must serve each parties legitimate interest in knowing what the investigation produced. Delay in providing the written outcome is not considered to be a neutral administrative matter. The *Sewell* decision demonstrates that an eighteen-day delay between verbal notification and written outcome, that was combined with ambiguity in the written outcome when it arrived, contributed directly to a finding of constructive dismissal. Timeliness is part of informational fairness, and informational fairness is a pillar of organisational justice that the investigation process must satisfy throughout, not only in the finding itself.

The bedrock principle that closes this chapter's argument is that a dismissal may be harsh, unjust or unreasonable notwithstanding the existence of a valid reason if the subsequent process is flawed. The Full Bench of the Fair Work Commission has stated this explicitly, and it is the principle that connects everything in this chapter to everything in Chapter Ten. The finding establishes the valid reason. It does not protect the employer from the consequences of a flawed show cause process. Both are required. Neither substitutes for the other.

PRACTITIONER NOTE

The finding failure most likely to produce a procedural challenge is the one that goes further than the evidence supports.

The specific form this takes is recognisable. The investigator believes, on the available evidence, that the conduct occurred. The finding establishes the conduct on the balance of probabilities. Then the finding continues: the respondent's behaviour reflects a pattern of disrespect, or demonstrates they are not suited to a position of trust, or shows a lack of integrity. Each of these additions is a characterisation the investigation's evidence does not establish. Each gives the respondent a ground to challenge the finding they would not have had if the finding had stopped at what the evidence shows.

Write the finding and then stop. What the evidence establishes is the finding. What the investigator believes about the respondent as a person is not, and the difference between these two things is the difference between a finding that survives challenge and one that does not.

The second failure is the finding recorded as not substantiated where the accurate record is unable to be determined. The evidence was not assessed and found insufficient. It was not gathered in a form that allowed assessment. The allegation was not resolved: it was abandoned at the point of conflict. Recording this as not substantiated implies an assessment was made and a standard applied. Recording it as unable to be determined is accurate. Accuracy about the limits of what the investigation produced is the obligation the finding carries.

The third failure is the finding that does not address the alternative explanation. The investigation that produces a finding of substantiated misconduct without any reference to the respondent's account, to what the strongest alternative explanation for the evidence was, and to why that alternative is less probable, has produced a document that cannot demonstrate the investigative standard was applied. It may be correct. It cannot be shown to be correct, and the distinction between those two things is the one the Fair Work Commission will draw.

A NOTE ON COGNITIVE STYLE

The finding-writing phase is the phase at which the pattern-recognition capacity of a non-linear thinker is most likely to produce a document that reflects the investigator's cognitive process rather than the evidential reasoning the finding requires.

The non-linear thinker who has reached a correct conclusion from a non-sequential reasoning process faces a specific writing challenge: the connections across evidence streams that produced the conclusion may not have followed the order the finding's structure requires. Translating a non-sequential cognitive process into a sequential analytical document is effortful, and the temptation is to begin with the conclusion and work back to the evidence that supports it. The finding that results reads as though the evidence was selected to support a conclusion already reached, because in a literal sense it was.

The structure in this chapter is the translation tool. Taking the six components in sequence, working through the allegation as particularised, the evidence relevant to each element, the weight assigned and why, the alternative considered and rejected, the conclusion that follows, and the policy or standard breach, produces the document the decision-maker needs even where the internal reasoning process did not proceed in that order. The structure is not a constraint on how the investigator thought. It is the form in which the reasoning is made visible and testable.

The investigation log, which records the decision-making process throughout the investigation, is the reference document at this stage. If the conclusion the finding reaches is consistent with the decisions recorded in the log, and if the alternative explanations recorded in the log have been addressed in the finding, the finding reflects the investigation's actual process rather than a reconstruction of it. The log is the protection against the backward construction problem. If the log does not support the finding, that is the information the investigator needs before the finding is finalised rather than after it is challenged.

What Comes Next

The finding is complete. The evidence has been assessed. The conclusion has been stated in terms the evidence supports. The alternative explanation has been addressed. The policy or standard breach has been assessed. The decision-maker has what they need to conduct the show cause process.

Chapter Nine addresses the investigation report: the document that records not just the findings but the process that produced them. The report is the evidence that the investigation was conducted to a standard. It will be read by people looking for reasons to challenge it, and it must be written knowing that every gap in its reasoning, every characterisation that exceeds what the evidence supports, and every ambiguity in its language is a point of vulnerability. The finding made with the discipline this chapter describes can survive that scrutiny. The report that records it must be written to the same standard.

Chapter Nine

Writing the Report

The investigation report is not a summary of what happened. It is the evidence that the investigation was conducted to a standard.

This distinction changes everything about how the report should be written. A summary of what happened is written for someone who needs to know the story. An investigation report is written for someone who is looking for reasons to challenge it: the respondent's legal representative, the Fair Work Commission, an internal appeals process, or a regulator conducting their own inquiry. Every section of the report must be written knowing it will be read by someone with a strong interest in finding it deficient, and that the deficiencies they find will determine the consequences for the organisation, the decision-maker, and the parties involved.

The corollary is that the report must not try to tell the whole story. The investigation report records what the investigation found and how it found it. The full narrative of every interview conducted, every document reviewed, every tangential matter that emerged and was set aside, does not belong in the report. What belongs is the finding, the process that produced it, and enough of the reasoning to demonstrate that the process met the standard. Completeness is not measured by volume. It is measured by whether the report answers the questions a fair-minded reviewer would ask.

The Purpose of the Report

The purpose of the investigation report is to demonstrate that the investigation met the standard and to transfer the findings to the decision-maker in a form they can act upon with confidence.

A sixty-page report is not an inquiry. It is a monument to the investigator's inability to find the real problem.

Before writing a single word, the investigator should hold three questions in mind that will govern every decision about what to include and how to express it.

The first question is: who is the reader? The immediate reader is the decision-maker, who needs to understand what was found, on what evidence, and to what standard, so they can conduct the show cause process that follows. The downstream readers are the parties themselves, their legal representatives, the Fair Work Commission if the matter proceeds, and potentially a court or regulator. The report must be written for the most demanding reader, not the most sympathetic one.

The second question is: what does the report need to demonstrate? That the investigation was conducted impartially, that the evidence was gathered through a reasonable process, that the findings were reached through reasoned assessment of that evidence, and that the alternative explanations were considered before the findings were made. The report is also the document that demonstrates the Fair Work Act's core objective was met: a fair go all round for both the employer and the employees involved. A report that cannot be assessed cannot demonstrate either the standard or the fairness.

The third question is: what must the report not do? It must not characterise the parties beyond what the evidence supports, narrate the investigation as a story, include evidence irrelevant to the findings, recommend a disciplinary outcome, or use language so guarded the findings cannot be understood. Each of these is a failure mode that recurs in workplace investigation reports and creates vulnerability regardless of the quality of the underlying investigation.

The Structure of the Report

A workplace investigation report that will survive Fair Work Commission scrutiny requires a defined architecture. The six sections that follow are not optional. Each serves a specific function in demonstrating that the investigation met the standard. Section 4 is the analytical core: it is where the six components of a finding from Chapter Eight are applied to each allegation in the report's defined form.

Section 1: Scope and Terms of Reference

The scope establishes the legal authority for the investigation. This section records the allegations investigated, the parties, the investigator's appointment and mandate, the relevant time period, and what was outside the scope. The scope section is a record of the pre-existing mandate. It does not define the mandate at the reporting stage: the Terms of Reference existed before the investigation began, and this section records them rather than creating them. A reviewer who questions whether the investigation had the authority to make a specific finding will look here first.

Section 2: Methodology

The methodology records the process by which the investigation was conducted. Who was interviewed, in what order, on what dates, and by what method. What documentary evidence was sought, from what sources, and by what process. What preservation requests were made and when. What the investigation log records about decisions of substance made during the process. A specific accuracy obligation applies here: where the methodology records that certain evidence was not pursued or that no witnesses were identified, that record must be factually accurate. Recording that no witnesses were identified when witnesses were identified by description but not located is not a finding about evidence. It is a false statement in the methodology. The *Smout* decision illustrates the consequence: the Commission found the investigator's claim that no witnesses had been identified was not accurate, and this contributed to the finding that the investigation lacked rigour.

Interviewees should be given the opportunity to review and sign off on the notes taken of their interviews before those notes are relied upon in the report. A signed record is more defensible than an unsigned one. Where a correction is made, both the original record and the correction should be preserved. Practitioners working from a structured interview protocol, including the Witness Interview Framework developed by The Analytical Studio, will already have this sign-off step built into the record template; practitioners without an existing template should incorporate it explicitly.

Section 3: Summary of Evidence

The summary of evidence records the evidence gathered, organised by allegation and by evidence category. It records what each piece of evidence shows, not what the investigator thinks it means. The characterisation of evidence belongs in the findings section, not here. The summary is the raw material. The findings section is the analysis.

The discipline that applies to this section is that witness accounts should be recorded in the witness's own language, clearly attributed, rather than in the investigator's reformulation. The investigator's paraphrase of a witness's account is the investigator's interpretation, and that interpretation may reflect the investigator's view of the case in ways invisible in the record.

A written chronology of the relevant events, drawn from the evidence gathered, is a useful analytical tool that can be annexed to the report. It provides the decision-maker and any downstream reviewer with a navigable timeline and makes contradictions in timing visible without requiring them to be embedded in the narrative.

Where evidence was gathered and assessed but not relied upon in reaching the findings, the report should record that the evidence was considered and explain why it was not given weight. The report that addresses only what was relied upon implies only what was relied upon mattered.

Non-essential documents should be held in a separate file available to the decision-maker if needed, rather than annexed to the report and cluttering the record. The report's annexures should contain the documents directly relied upon in the findings. Everything else is a supplementary file.

Section 4: Findings

The findings section is the analytical core of the report. The scope establishes what was asked. The methodology establishes how the evidence was gathered. The summary establishes what the evidence shows. The findings section answers the question the investigation was asked, using the six-component structure from Chapter Eight: the allegation as particularised, the evidence relevant to each element, the weight assigned and why, the alternative explanation considered and why it was not preferred, the conclusion on the balance of probabilities, and the assessment of whether the proven conduct constitutes a breach of the relevant standard. Each allegation receives this six-component treatment as a discrete sub-section. The structure is repeated for every allegation in the Terms of Reference, so that the analysis of each is fully self-contained.

Where the finding addresses a contested allegation, the findings section should accurately state the respondent's account and the strongest argument for the alternative before explaining why the evidence does not support it. This is not a courtesy to the respondent. It is the demonstration that the alternative was considered rather than ignored, and it is what distinguishes a defensible finding from an assertion dressed as one.

Section 5: Recommendations

The recommendations section records matters arising from the investigation that warrant attention beyond the disciplinary finding. Systemic issues identified during the investigation that may require a WHS response. Policy or process gaps the investigation has revealed. Referrals to other processes or authorities where the investigation has identified conduct outside its Terms of Reference that should be addressed separately.

A specific obligation belongs here that practitioners consistently overlook. Where the finding is not substantiated, the recommendations section must address whether an underlying work health and safety risk exists and requires control regardless of the disciplinary outcome. A not substantiated finding does not discharge the organisation's obligation to assess and control the conditions that gave rise to the complaint. The Model Code of Practice on Managing Psychosocial Hazards is explicit on this point, and the recommendations section is the appropriate place to record the assessment and any action required.

The recommendations section does not include a recommendation about disciplinary outcome. That is the decision-maker's function.

Section 6: Distribution and Confidentiality

The distribution list establishes who will receive the report and under what constraints. It should be defined before the report is finalised, not expanded after. The Charter of Human Rights and Responsibilities Act 2006 s.13 right to privacy and reputation applies to the report's distribution: every person who reads it beyond those with a legitimate need constitutes an interference with the privacy and reputation of the parties.

Where the report is intended to attract Legal Professional Privilege, all drafts and the final version must be marked strictly confidential and subject to Legal Professional Privilege before they are created. LPP can be lost if the report is distributed in a way inconsistent with the privilege. This is a decision for the commissioning authority, made before the investigation begins, and it must be reflected in every document the investigation produces from that point.

The privacy obligations that govern the report's handling differ depending on the parties' employment status. The Employee Record Exemption under the Privacy Act 1988 (Cth) applies to records used for employment-related purposes in relation to employees. It does not apply to non-employees, including contractors, clients, or members of the public who were involved in the investigation, for whom privacy obligations are more stringent. The report must treat the information of non-employee parties accordingly.

The Language of the Report

The report you write with excessive qualification today is the Fair Work Commission reversal you will explain to your CEO in six months.

The organising standard is captured in three Cs: complete, concise, and clear. Complete means all aspects of the investigation addressed and all issues resolved. Concise means direct, avoiding pretentious verbosity and the screenplay error of recounting everything the investigator was told rather than what the investigation found. Clear means coherent logic throughout, so the reasoning from evidence to finding is navigable by someone reading the report for the first time.

A single decision about point of view must be made before the report is drafted and maintained throughout. Third person, the investigator found, the complainant stated, is generally preferred for formal investigation reports because it creates appropriate distance between the investigator's observations and the findings. First person is acceptable where the investigator is recording a direct credibility observation, but it must be used consistently. A report that alternates between first and third person without reason signals a lack of structural control over the document.

Four language failures recur across workplace investigation reports.

The passive voice trap

Passive constructions used to avoid attributing conduct obscure the finding rather than protecting the parties. It was alleged that the complainant was subjected to comments of a sexual nature has removed the respondent from the conduct the finding addresses. The report records what the evidence shows about specific conduct by a specific person. Passive voice that obscures attribution produces a finding that cannot be understood or defended.

The vague finding

The balance of the evidence supports a conclusion that the conduct occurred tells the reader nothing about which evidence, why it was preferred, or what conduct was established. The finding must be specific.

The excessive qualification

The report written in language so guarded the finding cannot be determined has not discharged the investigator's function. The decision-maker cannot act on a finding that does not tell them what was established. The ambiguity a heavily qualified finding creates will be the vulnerability post-investigation challenge exploits.

The characterisation that exceeds the evidence

The report that describes the respondent as having shown a pattern of disrespect when the investigation addressed a single allegation has gone beyond what the evidence supports. Characterisations that exceed the finding's evidentiary foundation give the respondent grounds to challenge the finding that did not arise from the evidence itself.

The Minimum Report Architecture

Not every practitioner has access to structured report resources. Six documents constitute the minimum viable architecture for a defensible investigation report.

A scope and Terms of Reference template covering the allegations, the parties, the investigator's mandate, the relevant time period, and what is outside the scope. A methodology record template covering who was interviewed, in what order, on what dates, by what method, and what documentation was produced, including the sign-off record for each interview. An evidence matrix mapping each allegation to the evidence categories relevant to it, populated throughout the investigation. A finding structure template applying the six components from Chapter Eight to each allegation. A recommendations template separating systemic observations and WHS risk assessments from individual conduct findings. A distribution and storage record documenting who has received the report, when, and under what confidentiality obligations.

These six documents, developed before the investigation begins and populated throughout, are the investigation's administrative record. The report is written from these documents, not from the investigator's reconstruction of the investigation in retrospect. The quality of the report is determined by the quality of the process it records.

Practitioners working under sustained investigation volumes or in environments with significant external scrutiny may prefer a more developed framework than the minimum architecture provides. The Investigative Report Structuring Kit developed by The Analytical Studio is one such framework, designed for the structural translation problem described later in this chapter. Practitioners with access to other validated frameworks should use them. The framework matters less than the consistent application of the six-document architecture the report is built from.

Confidentiality, Privacy, and the Report's Limits

The investigation report contains personal information about people who have been involved in a formal process. The obligations governing its handling begin before it is finalised and continue long after it is distributed.

The collection and use of personal information during the investigation is governed by the Privacy Act 1988 (Cth) for private sector organisations and by the Privacy and Data Protection Act 2014 (Vic) for public sector organisations. The Charter of Human Rights and Responsibilities Act 2006 s.13 protects the right to privacy and reputation from unlawful or arbitrary interference. Collection must have been proportionate to the investigation's scope, and the report must be distributed only to those with a need for it.

The HRPA Practice Standard is specific: investigators cannot give absolute guarantees of confidentiality. The investigation report may be required to be produced in proceedings, and the parties are entitled to know this. A party told their account will be kept strictly confidential when the report may subsequently be disclosed has been misled, and the misrepresentation creates a procedural vulnerability independent of the report's content.

The report should be retained in accordance with the organisation's record-keeping obligations and applicable legislative requirements. It should be stored securely, accessed only by those with a need for it, and destroyed in accordance with the applicable retention schedule.

The Assessable Report

The principle that closes this chapter's argument is one the Fair Work Commission has applied consistently: it will not give weight to an investigation report it cannot assess.

An investigation report that summarises rather than records, that characterises rather than analyses, that arrives at conclusions without the reasoning that supports them, does not protect the employer's decision when it is challenged. The Commission will make its own findings from the evidence presented at hearing, without the benefit of the investigation's conclusions, and the employer who relied on a report that did not meet the standard will bear the consequences of that reliance.

The practical lesson is not that the report must be exhaustive. It is that the report must be assessable: a reviewer reading it must be able to determine what evidence was gathered, how it was assessed, what the findings were and on what basis, and what the alternative explanations were and why they were not preferred. A report that can be assessed on these questions can be defended. A report that cannot is not an investigation report at the standard. It is the appearance of one.

PRACTITIONER NOTE

The report-writing failure most likely to be invisible to the person who wrote it is the summary that substitutes for analysis.

The investigator who has lived with the investigation for weeks understands what the report says. They can see the reasoning in the summary because they know the reasoning. The reader who was not present cannot see the reasoning in the summary because it is not there. They see the conclusion the investigator reached. They cannot see how it was reached or whether the process that produced it was sound.

The finding must record the evidence, the weight, the alternative, and the conclusion in sequence. The shortcut that seems obvious in the context of weeks of investigation work is the gap that produces a challenge the report cannot answer.

The second failure is the report that recounts the investigation's narrative rather than its findings. The report that takes the reader through every interview, every document, and every decision made during the investigation is not demonstrating the standard. It is demonstrating the volume of work done. Volume is not the standard. The standard is whether the process was reasonable and the findings were defensible. A report that answers those two questions in twenty pages is more defensible than one that fails to answer them in sixty.

The third failure is the confidentiality breach built into the distribution. The report is finalised. The decision-maker receives it. Someone forwards it to the relevant manager. The relevant manager discusses the findings with their team. The parties learn through informal channels what the investigation produced before they have been formally notified. This is a procedural failure, a confidentiality breach, and a potential Charter violation in a single act. The distribution list is defined before the report is finalised. It does not expand without a documented reason.

A NOTE ON COGNITIVE STYLE

Report writing is the phase of the investigation that most directly exposes the gap between the investigator's cognitive process and the linear, sequential structure the report requires.

The non-linear thinker who has absorbed the full evidence base across weeks of investigation holds the picture in an integrated form: the connections between evidence streams, the pattern the individual pieces produce together, the conclusion the whole picture supports. The report requires that picture to be disassembled and reassembled in a defined sequence that may not reflect the order in which the connections were made.

The curse of knowledge from Chapter Eight applies with force here. Once the investigator knows the evidence, they cannot easily imagine the conclusion is not equally obvious to a reader encountering the investigation for the first time. The investigator who assumes the reader can see the reasoning because the reasoning feels self-evident skips the written steps that make it visible. The report that results is right in its conclusions and invisible in its reasoning. The investigation log, which has recorded the decision-making process throughout, is the bridge: the report's reasoning should be traceable to the log rather than reconstructed from memory.

A structured framework for the integrated-to-sequential translation reduces the effort the translation requires. The Investigative Report Structuring Kit developed by The Analytical Studio is one such framework; the section-by-section template described in this chapter performs the same function for practitioners working without a dedicated tool. The principle in either case is the same: the structure does not constrain the cognitive process. It externalises the discipline of presenting that process in the form the report requires.

The writing phase also benefits from the same structural brake applied throughout the investigation. Before the report is submitted, the investigator should ask whether a reviewer with no prior knowledge of the investigation could read the report and determine, from the report alone, what evidence was gathered, how it was assessed, what the findings were, and why the alternative explanations were rejected. If the answer is no, the report is not finished.

What Comes Next

The report is complete. The findings are stated in terms the evidence supports. The reasoning is visible. The alternative explanations have been addressed. The decision-maker has what they need.

Chapter Ten addresses what happens after the report is delivered: the show cause process, the outcome communication to both parties, the post-investigation obligations to the complainant, and the systemic review that the investigation's findings may have made necessary. The report is the end of the investigation. It is the beginning of the post-investigation obligations the organisation must discharge before the matter can be considered resolved.

Chapter Ten

Managing the Outcome

The investigation report is delivered. The finding is clear. The process was sound. The conclusion is defensible. And then the organisation does something that undoes it.

The handover of the investigation report is the point of maximum organisational risk.

Not because something will necessarily go wrong. Because this is the point at which the disciplines that governed the investigation, the structured process, the evidence standard, the procedural framework, are handed to a decision-maker who may not have been present for any of it, and who must now apply their own independent judgment in a process that has its own obligations and its own failure modes. The investigation that was conducted rigorously produces an unfair dismissal finding because of what happened in the six days after the report was handed over: the show cause meeting compressed to suit a deadline the investigation was never told about, the outcome letter that arrived weeks after the verbal notification, the complainant told the matter had been dealt with and then required to walk back into the same work area as the person she had accused, with no separation arrangement and no explanation of what dealt with meant.

The Fair Work Commission has been direct about this. A dismissal may be harsh, unjust or unreasonable notwithstanding the existence of a valid reason. The finding establishes the valid reason. It does not protect the employer from the consequences of a flawed post-investigation process. The core objective of the Fair Work Act, established in s.381(2), is ensuring a fair go all round for both employer and employee. The post-investigation process is where that objective is either demonstrated or abandoned. Both the investigation and the process that follows it are required. Neither substitutes for the other.

The natural counterargument is that operational urgency sometimes makes a compressed post-investigation process unavoidable. The Fair Work Commission has answered this directly in *Roy Smout v BHP Coal Pty Ltd* [2024] FWC 2062: operational urgency, a long weekend, and a mine divestment deadline did not override the respondent's right to a genuine show cause process. The Commission's reasoning was blunt. Union officials and HR staff are sometimes required to work outside normal hours. The convenience of the organisation does not override the respondent's right to a genuine process.

This chapter addresses the obligations that begin when the report is delivered and do not end until the organisation has discharged every one of them.

The Fact-Finder and the Decision-Maker

Chapter One drew a structural distinction that the rest of the handbook has assumed without restating: the investigator is a fact-finder, the decision-maker is a separate person, and the disciplinary outcome is the decision-maker's function rather than the investigator's. Chapters Eight and Nine returned to this in the context of the finding and the report. Chapter Ten is where the distinction operationally bites, because this is the stage at which the decision-maker takes over.

The transfer is the most consequential structural moment of the post-investigation period. The investigator hands over a report containing findings of fact assessed at the civil standard. The decision-maker receives the report and must now apply their own independent judgment to determine what action, if any, those findings warrant. The two roles are separate. The two judgments are separate. Conflating them, by allowing the investigator's view of the appropriate outcome to influence the decision-maker's assessment, or by allowing the decision-maker to substitute their own view of the facts for the findings the investigation produced, compromises both functions.

The practical implications follow. The investigator does not recommend a disciplinary outcome in the report. The decision-maker does not revisit the factual findings, which were assessed by the person who heard the evidence. The decision-maker takes the findings as given and assesses the appropriate response in light of them and of the wider circumstances the findings did not address. Where the decision-maker disagrees with a finding, the appropriate course is to commission further investigation rather than to overturn the finding informally. Where the investigator believes a particular outcome is warranted, the appropriate course is to articulate the seriousness of the conduct in the report's recommendations section without recommending the disciplinary response, which belongs to the decision-maker.

The Show Cause Process

A thirty-minute show cause meeting scheduled for a Friday afternoon is not an invitation to respond. It is a request for the respondent to witness their own dismissal.

The show cause process is a substantive procedural fairness obligation that the investigation's finding does not discharge. The investigation gave the respondent an opportunity to respond to the allegations. The show cause process gives the respondent an opportunity to respond to the proposed action taken in response to those findings. These are different obligations and neither satisfies the other.

The show cause process has three elements, each of which must be genuine rather than performed.

Notification of the proposed action

The respondent must be told, in writing, what action the decision-maker is proposing to take and why. The why is not a restatement of the investigation's findings. It is the decision-maker's own assessment of why those findings warrant the proposed action. The decision-maker must apply their own judgment to the findings, in light of all relevant circumstances, to reach the proposed outcome. That judgment must be visible in the notification.

A genuine opportunity to respond

The respondent must have adequate time to consider the proposed action, seek advice from a union official or legal representative if they wish, reflect on any mitigating circumstances they want to raise, and prepare a considered response. *Smout* established what this means: BHP's normal show cause process provided for seven days to respond in writing to a written show cause letter. Compressing this to a verbal notification meeting followed by dismissal thirty minutes later did not provide a full opportunity to respond.

The psychological mechanism behind the pre-determined outcome failure is worth naming because it is the mechanism practitioners most often do not recognise in their own process. Once a decision-maker has drafted the termination letter, or sought approval to terminate before the show cause meeting occurs, they experience pressure to behave consistently with that prior commitment. The show cause meeting becomes a sequence they must complete rather than a process that might produce a different outcome. The Commission has found exactly this pattern: the decision had already been made, the meeting was a mechanical sequence, and the respondent's response could not have changed the outcome because the outcome had already been determined. That is not a show cause process. It is the performance of one, and the performance no longer passes scrutiny.

For respondents who are neurodivergent, the show cause obligation is more demanding, not less. A respondent with non-linear working memory differences who is given a five to ten minute verbal notification and asked to respond on the spot has been denied a meaningful opportunity to respond regardless of the formal adequacy of the procedure. The obligation to allow adequate time applies with greater force where the respondent's capacity to process information and formulate a response requires more of it.

Genuine consideration of the response

The decision-maker must read and consider the response before finalising the outcome. The Commission's findings in *Smout* identified the features that mark a process as having failed this requirement: the termination letter drafted before the response was received, the script provided to the decision-maker with the dismissal section already highlighted, the response meeting reconvened within minutes of the response being given. Where these features are present, the decision-maker's consideration of the response is a procedural fiction.

The respondent's right to a support person at the show cause meeting is governed by s.387(d) of the Fair Work Act. Any refusal to allow a support person is a factor the Commission must take into account. The support person is for emotional support and as a sounding board. They are not legal representation and they do not answer questions on behalf of the respondent. Their attendance must be recorded.

For an action taken in response to a substantiated finding to attract the protection of reasonable management action under the Stop Bullying Benchbook, the action must be carried out in a reasonable manner. A show cause process that is compressed, pre-determined, or conducted without adequate notice strips the employer of that protection regardless of whether the underlying finding was sound.

The Decision

The decision about what action to take in response to the investigation's findings is the decision-maker's alone.

The decision is not a function of the finding. A finding of substantiated serious misconduct does not mandate dismissal. The decision-maker must assess the conduct found, the respondent's length of service and employment history, any mitigating circumstances the respondent has raised, the consistency of the proposed action with how similar conduct has been treated, the proportionality of the proposed action to the conduct established, and any other matters relevant to the fairness of the outcome. A finding of serious misconduct creates what Kahneman's research on the halo effect describes precisely: a global negative impression that can cause the decision-maker to discount mitigating factors, treating length of service, clean disciplinary history, and genuine remorse as obstacles to the conclusion the finding appears to demand, rather than as factors that must be assessed on their merits. The decision-maker who does not actively assess mitigating circumstances has not made a defensible decision. They have made a conclusion.

Dismissal is one available outcome where misconduct is substantiated. A warning, a final warning, a demotion, a transfer, a requirement to undertake training: these are available responses depending on the nature and severity of the conduct. The decision-maker who does not consider the available range of responses has not exercised the independent judgment their role requires.

A specific consideration applies to findings of single-incident unreasonable conduct. The Stop Bullying Benchbook establishes that conduct meets the legal threshold for bullying only if it is repeated. A finding of a single incident of unreasonable conduct does not meet that threshold. The decision-maker assessing the outcome for single-incident unreasonable conduct must consider the available responses against the conduct actually established rather than the conduct the finding might have implied if the threshold had been met.

Where the decision is to dismiss, the dismissal must be procedurally complete: notice or pay in lieu, payment of all accrued entitlements, confirmation of any post-employment obligations, and provision of the

Employee Assistance Program. These are not administrative details. Their absence creates liability independent of the investigation's quality.

Communicating the Outcome

The notification you delay by two weeks is the compensation order you will explain to your Board.

Both parties are owed a written outcome, in clear terms, without delay. The communication is the moment at which the investigation's procedural integrity is either confirmed or undone in the eyes of the people whose working lives it has affected. A finding that was reached through a defensible process and then communicated through silence, ambiguity, or delay produces the same procedural exposure as a finding that was never properly reached, because the people affected experience the outcome through the communication rather than through the process that produced it.

Communicating with the respondent

The written outcome to the respondent must state what the investigation found, what action is being taken and why, what the respondent's rights are in relation to any appeal or review, and what the next steps are. It must not characterise the respondent beyond what the finding supports, attribute motivations or intentions that were not the subject of the investigation, or make statements that exceed what the evidence established.

Where the outcome is dismissal, the respondent is entitled to a separation that preserves their dignity. The manner of the dismissal, how they are notified, whether they are permitted to farewell colleagues, whether personal belongings are collected privately, whether any announcement is made to their team, is not operationally neutral. The psychosocial hazard code of practice identifies the manner in which employment ends as a potential source of harm. The organisation has a duty to manage that process proportionately and with respect for the person.

Communicating with the complainant

The obligation to advise the complainant of the outcome is a procedural fairness requirement. The complainant is entitled to know whether their complaint was investigated, what the outcome was in general terms, and what steps, if any, have been taken in response. They are not entitled to know the specific disciplinary action taken against the respondent, the content of the respondent's show cause response, or other information that belongs to the respondent's privacy.

That boundary is not a practical challenge to be navigated with vague language. It is a defined line between what the complainant's procedural fairness requires and what the respondent's privacy right protects. The complainant who is told the matter has been dealt with has not been given what they are owed. The complainant who is told the specific disciplinary outcome has received information about another person's employment that belongs to that person. The communication that tells the complainant what they are entitled to know, that their complaint was taken seriously, that it was assessed against the applicable standard, what general outcome the assessment produced, and what measures have been put in place to address the workplace conditions it revealed, is both what the law requires and what basic dignity demands.

What the dnata case demonstrates

The *Courtney Sewell v dnata Airport Services Pty Limited* [2025] FWC 2823 decision illustrates how communication failures across both parties operate together to produce a constructive dismissal outcome. The investigation found the sexual harassment allegations not substantiated. The verbal outcome was communicated on 10 April 2025. The written outcome letter did not follow until 28 April 2025, only after the complainant requested it. The letter described the findings as unable to make a finding for some of the allegations, language so ambiguous the complainant could not determine whether her complaint had been assessed or dismissed. Her request to be rostered separately from the alleged harasser was refused. No workable return-to-work arrangement was provided. The Commission found constructive dismissal and awarded $36,468.39 in compensation, assessed using the Sprigg formula the Commission applies in unfair dismissal compensation matters.

The investigation itself was not the failure. What followed it was, and the failure operated through the communication: delayed, ambiguous, and not accompanied by the operational measures the complainant needed to return to a workplace she had been required to share with the person she had accused. The case is the clearest available statement that the post-investigation communication and the post-investigation safety obligations are not administrative tidy-ups. They are the substance of how the investigation lands on the people inside it.

Post-Investigation Safety Obligations

The investigation's finding does not discharge the organisation's work health and safety obligations.

The Model Code of Practice on Managing Psychosocial Hazards states this explicitly: where breaches of a code of conduct or policy are not proven there may still be an underlying work health and safety risk which needs to be controlled. A not substantiated finding does not close the WHS question. In some circumstances it intensifies it.

Where the investigation found the conduct not substantiated, the organisation must assess whether the conditions that gave rise to the complaint represent an ongoing psychosocial hazard requiring control regardless of the disciplinary outcome. A workplace in which a complainant does not feel safe to return, in which the power dynamics that produced the complaint remain unchanged, or in which the conditions that prevented earlier reporting still exist, has a psychosocial hazard the not substantiated finding has not resolved.

Where the investigation found the conduct substantiated, the post-investigation WHS obligations are specific. The complainant must be able to return to a safe working environment. Where the respondent remains employed, that may require temporary separation arrangements, changes to reporting lines, or other measures to ensure the complainant is not required to work alongside or report to the person whose conduct toward them has been established. The complainant's safety in the workplace is a separate obligation from the disciplinary finding, and a failure to address it can produce a constructive dismissal outcome regardless of what the investigation found about the individual conduct.

The PCBU's primary duty of care under s.19 of the Work Health and Safety Act 2011 (Cth) requires the elimination or minimisation of psychosocial risks as far as is reasonably practicable. That duty does not end when the investigation report is filed. It continues through the post-investigation period and through the return-to-work arrangements.

Concurrent External Processes and the Referral Obligation

The investigation's completion does not resolve the question of whether external processes have been or should be triggered by what the investigation found. The mapping exercise the practitioner conducted at the preliminary assessment stage in Chapter Two now returns as a closing obligation, applied to what the investigation has actually established.

Where the conduct established meets a threshold for external jurisdiction, the obligation to refer is independent of whether the parties have done so. Where the conduct may constitute a criminal offence, police should be informed regardless of the internal disciplinary outcome. Where the conduct constitutes a notifiable WHS incident under the relevant Act, the reporting obligation applies and is not satisfied by the internal investigation having addressed the matter. Where the conduct triggers mandatory reporting obligations under sector-specific frameworks, those obligations operate on their own timeline.

Where an external process is already underway in relation to the same conduct, the practitioner must address the structural questions that arise from the interaction. The internal investigation's findings may be required to be produced in the external proceeding. The use to which those findings can be put depends on the standards the external forum applies, which are not always equivalent to the civil standard the internal investigation applied. Confidentiality frameworks differ between organisational policy and statutory schemes, and information shared with an external body may carry obligations or protections the internal investigation cannot assume. Where these interactions are unclear, specific advice should be sought before information is shared in either direction.

Where the investigation has revealed conduct outside the original Terms of Reference that engages an external jurisdiction, the recommendations section of the investigation report should identify the referral and the basis for it. The referral itself, the date it was made, and the body to which it was made should be documented in the investigation file.

For public sector practitioners, the post-investigation period may also engage the integrity commission, ombudsman, freedom of information, and public interest disclosure frameworks that apply to the relevant agency. The interactions are complex and beyond the scope of the standard methodology this handbook describes. Where these frameworks are likely to be engaged, specific advice should be sought from the organisation's legal and integrity advisers before the investigation file is closed.

The Systemic Review

Most investigations close when the finding is communicated and the disciplinary process is complete. The obligation most investigations do not discharge is the systemic review: the organisation's assessment of what the investigation revealed about its own conditions, and what those conditions require the organisation to do beyond the resolution of the individual matter.

The systemic review addresses four questions.

What conditions made this conduct possible, or allowed it to continue unreported until it reached the threshold of a formal complaint? The investigation that has run properly will have gathered evidence bearing on this question even if it was not what the Terms of Reference asked. Power dynamics, management practices, the organisation's response to prior complaints, cultural norms that normalise or minimise certain conduct: these are the conditions the systemic review must assess.

What policy or process gaps did the investigation reveal? An investigation that proceeded because the organisation had no early intervention process, no clear complaint pathway, or no policy covering the conduct alleged has revealed gaps the investigation's resolution does not fill.

What management or supervisory failures contributed to the conduct or to the conditions in which it occurred? A finding of individual misconduct is not necessarily a finding that the individual acted alone in the relevant sense. Where a manager knew or should have known about the conduct and did not act, or where the reporting structure created conditions in which the conduct was possible, the systemic review must address this.

What must the organisation do to ensure the conditions that produced this complaint are not reproduced? The systemic review's output is not a list of observations. It is a set of concrete actions with owners and timelines drawn from the investigation's findings and recommendations.

The mandatory consultation obligation under s.35 of the Occupational Health and Safety Act 2004 (Vic) and s.47 of the Work Health and Safety Act 2011 (Cth) applies to this review. Where the systemic review identifies a psychosocial hazard, the organisation must allow affected workers a reasonable opportunity to express their views on how that hazard will be controlled. The systemic review is not a management exercise conducted in isolation from the people whose work environment it addresses.

Post-Investigation Record-Keeping

The investigation record must be retained in accordance with the organisation's record-keeping obligations and applicable legislative requirements.

The investigation file should be held securely, accessible only to those with a need for it, for the period required by the applicable retention schedule. The Fair Work Act 2009 requires employment records to be kept for seven years. Practitioners should confirm the applicable requirement for their jurisdiction and organisation type, as some public sector instruments and industry-specific regulations impose different periods. For matters that have produced Fair Work Commission applications, the record must be retained for the duration of any proceedings and for a period after they conclude.

The investigation file should contain the complete record: the Terms of Reference, the investigation plan, the evidence matrix, the interview records with sign-offs, the investigation log, the full report, and all documents relied upon in reaching the findings. Documents gathered but not relied upon should be held in the supplementary file but must be retained. They may be required if the finding is challenged. The distribution record must be maintained as part of the file. Where a post-investigation referral was made, the referral and its basis must be documented.

Once the retention period has expired, the investigation file should be destroyed in accordance with the applicable schedule. A file retained beyond its purpose is a privacy risk for the parties it describes, and the obligation to destroy records at the end of their retention period is as much a legal obligation as the requirement to retain them during it.

The Lessons Learned Loop

Every investigation produces information about what worked and what did not. This information is most useful immediately after the investigation closes, before the lessons degrade under the weight of the next operational priority.

A brief post-investigation review, conducted against the investigation's process rather than its findings, produces the learning that makes the next investigation better. What planning decisions would have produced a stronger evidence base? What sequencing decisions created the most risk? What communication failures created the most procedural vulnerability? What would the investigation have done differently if it had known at the outset what it knew at the end?

This review is not a performance assessment of the investigator. It is the organisation's investment in the quality of its next investigation. The organisation that never asks these questions after an investigation closes produces the same failures under different circumstances for years.

PRACTITIONER NOTE

The post-investigation failure most likely to produce a challenge is the show cause process that went through the motions.

The specific experience from investigative and prosecutorial practice is that this failure is recognisable by a single feature: the decision had already been made before the show cause meeting was scheduled. The termination letter was drafted. Approval to terminate had been sought and received before the meeting occurred. The script provided to the decision-maker had the dismissal section already highlighted. The meeting was scheduled before a long weekend, at the end of a process that had been compressed by a deadline the investigation was never told about.

The Commission sees this pattern with frequency. It does not require the investigation to have been flawed to find the dismissal unfair. It requires only that the respondent was not given the genuine opportunity the Act mandates. An investigation that met every standard can produce an unfair dismissal finding at the show cause stage, and that is the failure the practitioner is most often not thinking about when they hand over the report and consider their work complete.

The work is not complete when the report is delivered. It is complete when the show cause process has been conducted, the decision has been made by the decision-maker on the full circumstances, the outcomes have been communicated to both parties in writing without delay, the post-investigation safety obligations have been addressed, any external referral obligations have been discharged, and the systemic review has produced actions with owners and timelines. Until each of these has been done, the investigation's exposure to challenge remains open.

The second failure is the complainant communication that defaults to silence. The organisation that concludes its obligations to the complainant when the disciplinary decision is made has not understood what those obligations are. A complainant who made a complaint at personal risk, participated in the investigation at personal cost, and is told only that the matter has been resolved is not being treated with the dignity the process owes them. They may lodge a general protections claim not because the investigation produced the wrong finding but because the organisation's handling of them after the finding communicated that their complaint was an inconvenience rather than a matter taken seriously.

For practitioners in council HR teams and small public sector agencies, the post-investigation period engages additional obligations the standard methodology does not address: freedom of information disclosure timelines, public interest disclosure follow-up, integrity commission notification thresholds, and the specific record-keeping obligations of the Local Government Act or its equivalents. The practitioner who has applied the post-investigation checklist as drafted but has not assessed these additional obligations has discharged the standard but not the jurisdiction.

A NOTE ON COGNITIVE STYLE

The post-investigation phase is the phase at which the cognitive demands of the investigation have been highest for the longest period, and at which the practitioner is most at risk of missing the steps that matter most.

The investigation log and the post-investigation checklist are the tools for this phase. The checklist externalises the obligations that must be met: the show cause process steps, the written outcome communications for both parties, the post-investigation safety assessment, the external referral assessment, the record-keeping obligations, the systemic review trigger. Each item is confirmed when it is completed.

The specific risk for a non-linear thinker is not that the obligations are unknown. It is that the investigation's resolution produces a cognitive release that feels like completion. The file has been handed over. The finding has been communicated. The operational pressure that drove the investigation's timeline has eased. This reduction in cognitive load signals, at the System 1 level, that the work is done. It is not. The post-investigation checklist held as a standing document, opened at the point of report delivery and closed only when every item is confirmed, is the difference between a managed close and an open exposure.

What the Investigation Was For

This chapter is the last in a sequence that began with the investigative standard in Chapter One. Naming what the sequence has been building toward belongs in the closing pages.

The investigative standard exists not to protect organisations from litigation, though it does that. Not to produce findings that satisfy the Fair Work Commission, though it produces those too. It exists because the people inside a workplace investigation are people whose working lives, reputations, and psychological health may be permanently altered by what the process produces. A complainant who made a report about conduct that harmed them deserves a process that took that harm seriously. A respondent who is the subject of an allegation deserves a process that presumed nothing and proved what it found. Witnesses who were asked to give an account of what they observed deserved a process that protected their participation and used their evidence with the care it required.

The practitioner who conducts the investigation is also one of the people inside it. The handbook has addressed this in earlier chapters at the points where it most affects the work: the bias rule as the external scaffolding that lets the investigator refuse a predetermined outcome, the management of interview density across a sustained programme, the alternative hypothesis test as the structural support that lets a finding be made by reference to a method rather than to personal certainty. The point that those chapters made in their own contexts can now be made in its general form. The investigative standard is not sustainable on individual courage. It is sustainable because the method is external to the person applying it, because the structure protects the judgment, and because the practitioner who is asked to do this work over years can do it without burning out or compromising the standard on the matters where the pressure runs highest. That is what the handbook's structural elements are for, and it is also what makes the work bearable as a programme rather than as a single matter.

Chapter One closed on the line that the chapters that follow would build the scaffolding the standard requires. The scaffolding is now built. The Terms of Reference, the investigation plan, the evidence matrix, the cognitive interview methodology, the credibility framework, the alternative hypothesis test, the six-component finding architecture, the six-section report structure, the post-investigation checklist that this chapter closes on: each was constructed in its own chapter, and together they are what makes the standard sustainable in practice rather than only available in principle. The handbook does not produce findings. The practitioner does. The handbook provides the structure that lets the practitioner produce them defensibly, repeatedly, and across the range of matters they will encounter without depending on the personal capacity that would otherwise have to carry the work alone.

The investigation that meets the standard this handbook has described is not a bureaucratic exercise that happens to comply with the Fair Work Act. It is a process conducted by a practitioner who understood what was at stake for the people inside it, including themselves, and who brought the same standard to every step that they would want applied if the process were being conducted about them.

That is the investigative standard. Everything else in this handbook is the methodology for meeting it.

Further Reading

The handbook draws on a body of legislation, regulatory guidance, judicial and tribunal decisions, and research in cognitive and health psychology. The references below are organised by category for practitioners who wish to consult the source material directly.

LEGISLATION

Fair Work Act 2009 (Cth).

Work Health and Safety Act 2011 (Cth).

Occupational Health and Safety Act 2004 (Vic).

Privacy Act 1988 (Cth).

Privacy and Data Protection Act 2014 (Vic).

Charter of Human Rights and Responsibilities Act 2006 (Vic).

Sex Discrimination Act 1984 (Cth).

Local Government Act 2020 (Vic).

REGULATORY GUIDANCE AND CODES OF PRACTICE

Safe Work Australia. Model Code of Practice: Managing Psychosocial Hazards at Work.

Fair Work Commission. Anti-Bullying Benchbook.

Fair Work Commission. Unfair Dismissals Benchbook.

Australian Human Resources Institute. HR Practice Standards.

FAIR WORK COMMISSION DECISIONS

Courtney Sewell v dnata Airport Services Pty Limited [2025] FWC 2823.

Roy Smout v BHP Coal Pty Ltd [2024] FWC 2062.

Practitioners should refer to the Fair Work Commission's decision database at fwc.gov.au for the full text of these decisions and for more recent authority on the questions they address.

COGNITIVE AND HEALTH PSYCHOLOGY

Camerer, C., Loewenstein, G., and Weber, M. (1989). The curse of knowledge in economic settings: An experimental analysis. *Journal of Political Economy*, 97(5), 1232–1254.

Fisher, R. P., and Geiselman, R. E. (1992). *Memory-Enhancing Techniques for Investigative Interviewing: The Cognitive Interview*. Springfield, IL: Charles C. Thomas Publisher.

Kahneman, D. (2011). *Thinking, Fast and Slow*. New York: Farrar, Straus and Giroux.

Ross, L. (1977). The intuitive psychologist and his shortcomings: Distortions in the attribution process. In L. Berkowitz (Ed.), *Advances in Experimental Social Psychology* (Vol. 10, pp. 173–220). New York: Academic Press.

Tversky, A., and Kahneman, D. (1973). Availability: A heuristic for judging frequency and probability. *Cognitive Psychology*, 5(2), 207–232.

Tversky, A., and Kahneman, D. (1974). Judgment under uncertainty: Heuristics and biases. *Science*, 185(4157), 1124–1131.

Wason, P. C. (1960). On the failure to eliminate hypotheses in a conceptual task. *Quarterly Journal of Experimental Psychology*, 12(3), 129–140.

Yerkes, R. M., and Dodson, J. D. (1908). The relation of strength of stimulus to rapidity of habit-formation. *Journal of Comparative Neurology and Psychology*, 18(5), 459–482.

METHODOLOGY SOURCE MATERIAL

The Davies Diagnostic. The Analytical Studio. The methodological foundation of this series, addressing the gap between stated problems and the real problems organisations need to solve.

About the Author

Benjamin Davies is a practitioner with fourteen years of investigative and prosecutorial experience and a Master of Human Resource Management. He works at the intersection of investigative methodology, organisational psychology, and the regulatory frameworks within which Australian workplace practice operates.

His work draws on a career spent applying evidential standards to complex matters under institutional pressure, and translates the disciplines that produce defensible findings in formal investigative contexts into a methodology that practitioners can apply to the workplace investigations they conduct as part of their professional practice.

He is the founder of The Analytical Studio, an evidence-based operational consulting practice serving leaders, HR practitioners, investigators, and local government officers across Victoria, Australia.

About The Analytical Studio

The Analytical Studio is an evidence-based operational consulting practice. Its work rests on a single observation: the problem stated is rarely the problem that matters, and finding the real one is where this practice begins.

Most organisations already know something is wrong. The difficult part is not finding a problem, it is being willing to look clearly at it when the answer is inconvenient, and then building the solution with enough rigour that it holds up once it is implemented. The Studio exists because the gap between what organisations know and what they are able to act on is almost always a methodology problem, not a resource problem. The tools, frameworks, and consulting practice it offers are built to close that gap, by applying the same evidential standards to operational problems that investigators apply to complex cases, and that scientists apply to contested questions.

The Studio's services include evidence-based operational consulting, structured methodologies and frameworks for HR practitioners and investigators, AI-augmented tools for complex analytical work, and professional resources for leaders, council officers, and small business owners working through the kinds of operational and investigative matters this handbook addresses.

Further information, additional resources, and contact details are available at theanalyticalstudio.com.au.

A NOTE TO THE READER

If this handbook has been useful to your practice, an honest review on Amazon helps other practitioners find it. Reviews do not need to be long. A sentence or two about what you found valuable is more useful to the next reader than a general endorsement. The methodology in this handbook will be enhanced in later iterations for having been used and tested by practitioners in the field. If you encounter a matter where the methodology did not hold up, or where something important was missing, I would like to know. You can reach me through theanalyticalstudio.com.au.

Made in the USA
Monee, IL
04 November 2026

67385357R00089